GUIDE 1
WRITING THE MYSTERY NOVEL

Lots of Examples Plus Dead Bodies

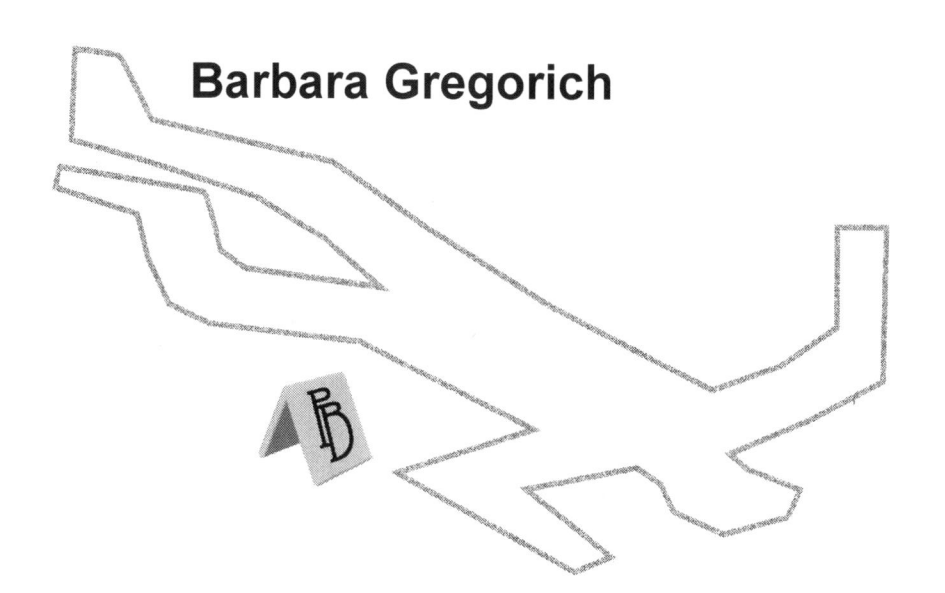

Barbara Gregorich

Copyright 2014 by Barbara Gregorich
All rights reserved, including the reproduction of the whole or any part of the contents without written permission from the author, except for reviewers, who may quote brief passages in a review.
Printed in the United States of America

ISBN-13: 978-1500714482
ISBN-10: 1500714488

Cover by Robin Koontz
Cover photo by Dm_Cherry/Shutterstock
Design by Robin Koontz
Index by Sharon Johnson

Gregorich, Barbara
Guide to Writing the Mystery Novel: Lots of Examples, Plus Dead Bodies
Philbar Books
Chicago, IL

For Robin Koontz,
who is always generous
in helping her friends
and fellow writers

Contents

Introduction		i
1	Plot, Character, and Setting	1
2	Plot	5
3	Naming Your Characters	16
4	Developing Major Characters — Motivation	30
5	Minor Characters	44
6	Character Tags	50
7	Setting, Including Scene of the Crime	57
8	Point of View	69
9	Summary, Scene, and Conflict	85
10	Subplots	93
11	Plot Complications	101
12	Casting Suspicion	106
13	Planting Clues	115
14	Disguising of Motive, Means, and Opportunity	122
15	Timelines	128
16	Rising Action, Pace, and Pacing	131
17	Exposition and Beginnings	143
18	When to Introduce the Villain	153
19	Foreshadowing	157
20	Dialogue	163
21	Description	173
22	Solution and Denouement	182
23	Outlining	191
24	Rewriting	197
25	Writing Well	201
Index		209

Introduction

Why, you may be asking yourself, should you read this book or trust its advice? It's not by Dennis Lehane, Sue Grafton, Michael Connelly, or any other bestselling mystery writer. What can somebody who's not a bestselling mystery writer possibly know that will help you write that mystery novel you've been yearning to start? Or maybe finish. Or maybe rewrite.

The answer is: Lots. Even though you probably haven't heard of me, I've been a writer for more than thirty years, and during that time I've published close to 200 books, many of them educational/instructional books. As a writer and a teacher of writing, I pay close attention to the process of writing — to what I need to know in order to write a certain kind of book, to the obstacles I face, to the decisions I need to make, the order I need to make them in, and the byproducts of all these processes. I've published two mystery novels (adult) and ghostwritten four Boxcar Children mysteries. The advice and suggestions I make in this book are based on three particulars: (1) the fact that I've been an avid reader of mysteries since I was eleven years old and have paid attention not only to what I like and don't like, but also to what works and what doesn't work for me as a reader; (2) the fact that, in writing my own mysteries, I paid attention to the decisions I had to make; (3) the fact that I greatly enjoy helping other people learn how to do something for themselves.

So that's why you might want to read this book and trust its advice.

Speaking of which, I've designed the chapters of this guide in such a way that you can read them in any order. While I think you will benefit most if you read from the beginning of the book to the end, I also recognize that you may want or need to know something in particular (subplots, say, or dialogue) immediately and will go directly to those chapters.

Throughout this guide I'll talk about the mystery novel both in general and in particular. For the particular, exact, see-what-I-did advice, I will use my second mystery, *Sound Proof*, as an example, with occasional forays into my first mystery, *Dirty Proof*. I will talk about characters in the book, give examples of how I hid clues, examples of how I threw suspicion onto innocent characters, examples of how I developed conflict, and so on and so forth. Because I want each chapter to stand on its own, I have occasionally repeated information and examples.

As you read this guide, you will learn which characters committed the three crimes in *Sound Proof*. If you think you want to read *Sound Proof* before you read this guide, the novel is available in softcover and ebook form.

I hope that this book, *Guide to Writing the Mystery Novel*, helps you in a myriad of ways.

1 Plot, Character, and Setting

You have probably heard of and maybe even participated in that never-ending chicken-egg debate writers have with one another. I call it a chicken-egg debate because it reminds me of the argument, *Which came first, the chicken or the egg?* In writing the debate is, *Which comes first, character or plot?* That is, which of these two helps you create your novel? Which do you think of first? Do you create your characters and then put them in a plot? Or do you create a plot, then invent characters to people it?

I always like to throw a wrench into the gears of this debate by asking, *What about setting?* Because for me, setting comes tied to both plot and character. In fact, for me, and I'm sure for many other writers, character, plot, and setting arrive at the door as a trio, arms linked.

Let me explain what I mean by that, using both *Dirty Proof* and *Sound Proof* as examples. During the 1970s I worked at the *Boston Globe*, the *Gary Post-Tribune*, and finally the *Chicago Tribune* as a typesetter. This was in the days of cold type, which in its various forms followed hot type, the latter referring to the slugs of molten lead cast by Linotype machines and locked into forms so that printing plates could be made for each page of a newspaper. The printing plates were wrapped around gigantic web presses, inked, and then the presses were put into rapid motion. Out spewed tens or hundreds of thousands of copies of each day's newspaper.

With the arrival of the cold type process, the old Linotype machines were bypassed, as were their molten slugs of lead. Instead, ordinary typewriters were used to produce copy: first on six-hole-punch paper tape, then with scanner-readable fonts on white paper. After personal computers arrived, reporters typed copy directly into word processing programs, bypassing the composing room altogether.

As I said, I worked in this environment in three different cities, and each day that I entered the work area I saw, heard, and smelled the gigantic web presses. Above these presses ran catwalks. Pressmen and mechanics stood on the catwalks, but occasionally I would notice a white-shirted, suited man (or several of them) standing there looking down at the presses. These suited men, I surmised, were newspaper executives.

When I and my fellow typesetters worked, we worked at a frantic pace: edition deadlines waited for no one. But nearly every day idle moments occurred while we waited for copy to arrive from the reporters, and during these idle moments I often speculated what would happen if somebody pushed a person off the catwalks into the spinning, pounding web presses. Let me rephrase that. I knew *what* would happen: instant death. But I wondered *why* somebody would murder in this manner. I wondered *who* they might murder. I wondered *how* they might cover it up. And I wondered *how* my detective would solve the crime.

Yes, I had a detective. He sprang to life the moment I began wondering about the crime. Here I must confess that I am a private-eye kind of woman. Perhaps this stems from the fact that I was an avid Sherlock Holmes fan by the time I was eleven years old, and when I began to read other mysteries, particularly those written in the Golden Age (roughly 1920-38), I again preferred private eyes. I read all of Christie and enjoyed the Miss Marple novels. But I *idolized* the Hercule Poirot novels: he was a professional.

Now, I'm not in any way saying that your hero must be a private eye. She or he could be a police detective. She or he could be an amateur. If so, then you'll have to put everything I say in this book into the context of your own experience reading police procedurals and/or amateur detective novels (cozies), for my examples will be about my protagonist, who is a private eye. While my hero, Frank Dragovic, might have difficulty with the police because he's not supposed to be investigating an active case (that is, one the police are working on), your police detective won't have that problem. Your amateur detective might. While my private eye might carry a gun, it's highly unlikely that an amateur detective would. And while a professional detective has had years of training in crime investigation, an amateur has not. This doesn't mean that an amateur can't apply skills of observation to a crime: she or he can certainly do that. Thinking skills aren't confined to professionally trained characters. A private eye will continue despite all odds because that is his job, whereas the reasons an amateur might persist are very different and have to be developed differently. More about these things in the chapter on character.

Back to my first mystery and the question of character, plot, and setting. I've given you the background: my work experience and my idle speculations about murder. If I tried to recreate how the idea that became *Dirty Proof* came to me, I would have to state it something like this: *A private detective (man) is asked by a typesetter (female) who works in the composing room of a Chicago newspaper to solve the crime of who pushed a newspaper executive to his death off the catwalks structured above the web presses — she wants him to solve the crime before the police can accuse her of committing it.*

As you can see, all three elements — character, plot, setting — came into my mind as one package. I didn't know who my characters were yet. Even though I had a glimmer of who the two main characters were, I hadn't thought about the other characters. And the two main characters had no names yet, no backstory, no size or shape or quirks. I did know parts of the plot (what the crime was), but I didn't know why. I didn't know who committed it. As for setting, I knew where this story took place. I knew the setting very well indeed.

To further illustrate how, for me, character and setting and plot arrive as a trio, I'll explain how I came to write *Sound Proof*, the sequel to *Dirty Proof*. My husband, Phil Passen, started to play the hammered dulcimer during the early 1990s. As a result we traveled to hammered dulcimer festivals in most of the states east of the Mississippi River. I'm not a musician, so during these festivals (some of which lasted a week) I usually read mysteries or worked on writing projects, or hiked, or just sat around and observed.

One of the things I observed was that some musicians were very rigid about who could or could not play with their group, even during informal evening jams. For some of these rigid people, common instruments such as the guitar, fiddle, and banjo were welcome, but uncommon instruments such as the bowed psaltry or hammered dulcimer were not welcome. As a result, an idea something like this came to me: *Frank Dragovic is attending a week-long old-time music festival at which a leading fiddler who has insulted just about everybody is murdered. The festival organizer hires Frank to solve the mystery.*

This time around I already had my protagonist, so naturally the idea came to me with "Frank Dragovic" instead of "a private detective." I knew what the crime was, although this time I didn't know how it was committed: not at first. I knew why the fiddler was killed, but I didn't know who did it. And, as before, I knew the setting well: it was, for me, a part of the plot and even part of the characters. For me, setting comes with my original idea. If setting doesn't come to you that way, you can learn to visualize setting better and to understand its importance later in this book.

If character and plot don't arrive at your doorstep as a duo, that's okay. We're all different, and what we create will be different, and the method we use to create it will reflect who we are and how we think. So if characters are what come to you first and exclusively, and you can't consider plot until you know your characters, that's fine. That's who you are and how you work.

Likewise if plot comes to you first and exclusively, and you can't consider characters until you have your plot worked out, that's also okay. That's who you are and how you think. In each case, don't worry about whether the idea knocking at your door is a trio, a duo, or a solo. It is what it is. Welcome it in, and begin to work.

Plot

A novel has to begin somewhere, and despite the never-ending debate over which comes first, character or plot, my guess is that when it comes to mystery writing, plot is what comes to mind first for most writers.

Plot is what came first to Earl Derr Biggers, successful writer of popular fiction during the 1910s. During a vacation to Hawaii in 1920, he was lying on the beach at Waikiki, observing what was happening around him, and, as he told his editor, he came up with an idea for "the perfect murder." Later, when Biggers sat down to write the story, he created the characters who peopled the book, including a character he thought of a quarter of the way into the book. That was Charlie Chan, Chinese-Hawaiian police detective.

Biggers wrote a total of six Chan novels before he died, and during those years (1924-1933) the novels were translated into dozens of languages. Chan became known around the world — indicating, I think, that even if a writer comes up with plot first, he can still create characters who become greater and better-known than any of the plots.

Plot may come first to you, or it may not. Regardless, I'm going to discuss plot first because it's the spine of your novel. More about spine later in this chapter.

If you played the game of Clue when you were a child, then you're familiar with the basic questions of plot: *who, how,* and *where.* If I recall Clue doesn't delve into *when*: but you as a mystery writer no doubt will, because *when* is tied to opportunity. When was the crime committed and who had the opportunity to commit it at that time?

25-Word Plot Summaries

The single most important element of plot is *conflict*. All fiction contains conflict. Without conflict, there is no drama: there is merely wandering from point to point. Sometimes pointlessly. Conflict can be as serious as armed struggle, as common as a major disagreement or argument, or as low-key as incompatibility between two different opinions.

In fiction the conflict is expressed through the protagonist (hero) and at least one of the following other "roles" — antagonist (villain, archenemy, etc.); mirror (a person who reflects what the hero wants, often with a difference); romance (the romantic interest of the hero). Sometimes, as in *Dirty Proof,* one character can represent more than one of these roles. In that novel Suzanne is both the mirror and the romance. In Dashiell Hammett's *The Maltese Falcon* Brigid O'Shaughnessy is both the romance and the antagonist. In *Sound Proof* Mary Ployd is both the mirror and an antagonist.

In classes on writing traditional novels (as opposed to episodic novels), writers are taught the skill of being able to summarize their story in twenty-five words or fewer. This summary can be used in query letters to agents and editors. It's also used in writing workshops and with writing coaches. Having such a summary helps a writer in two major ways: (1) it allows the writer to see that she does, in fact, have a plot that contains conflict; (2) it allows anybody interested in the book to grasp immediately the main conflict of the story.

Sometimes this 25-word statement is written out as a sentence. For example: **Ahab vows vengeance against the whale which bit off his leg and pursues it across the vast oceans, but the whale refuses to be caught.** That sentence, which comes to twenty-five words exactly, indicates that the main conflict in *Moby Dick* is between Ahab and the white whale. They are protagonist and antagonist. (If you disagree with this interpretation of the conflict in *Moby Dick,* you would then write the 25-word statement another way.)

Sometimes the conflict is stated in three lines, as follows:
**Ahab vows vengeance against the whale
but the whale refuses to be caught
and, instead, wrecks vengeance on Ahab**
In the three-line version, the last line is always the resolution:

the solution to the dispute.

Pulitzer-prize winning journalist Jon Franklin takes this three-line version even further when he teaches writing to college students, as explained in *Writing for Story*, his book on how to write dramatic nonfiction. Franklin tells writers that they must be able to state the conflict and resolution in three lines, each line containing only three words, each verb a strong verb.

Ahab pursues Moby
Moby eludes Ahab
Moby destroys Ahab

Elemental, isn't it? Basic. But of the utmost importance — this statement represents the spine of the author's story.

Franklin and many other teachers of writing believe (and I agree) that unless you are able to state the conflict of your story in such a manner, *you really don't know what the conflict is.* If you don't know what the conflict is, then you need to think and think and think, talk out loud to yourself, take notes, juggle notecards: do whatever it takes to help yourself construct a story with a viable plot. A plot that you understand and can summarize in twenty-five words or fewer. And you must be able to state that plot so that the first line represents what the hero wants or does, the second line states what the conflict or problem is, and the third line states the resolution.

Most writers, experienced or beginning, find this simple exercise incredibly difficult. That's usually because they don't know or aren't sure what the conflict in their novel is, or because they aren't able to separate out the main conflict from all the other things going on in the story. In order to write a gripping story, you need to both understand the conflict in your novel and be able to state it succinctly.

What Detective Heroes Want

Luckily for mystery writers, the hero in a mystery almost always wants one thing primarily: to solve the mystery. The mystery is usually who committed murder. It's true that you can write a mystery about who stole a $10 million painting, or who embezzled millions, or even who forged a historic document, or any other crimes that don't involve murder. But readers, at least American readers, really want murder mysteries, probably because the stakes are the highest.

The fact that in a mystery novel the protagonist's main want (and the want is what helps drive the action forward) is to solve the mystery, makes your job easier. On the first of your three lines, you write something like this:

Frank wants to discover who murdered Stubbs

Or, if you're going for Jon Franklin's three words per line with strong verbs, you write:

Frank seeks murderer

In fact, not only is the first line of your plot summary almost written for you, the second line is also easier to come up with than if you were writing a mainstream novel. It could be something like one of these:

but the killer has hidden his motives well

but the killer is someone Frank does not suspect

but the killer used a cat's paw to commit the murder

but the killer has set a deadly trap for whoever gets close to the solution

In coming up with that second line, you are making a major plot decision that you will have to follow through with in the writing.

Now comes the third and final line of your basic plot summary. Because the first line is **Frank wants to discover who murdered Stubbs,** the resolution can be one of only two things. Either **Frank finds who the killer is,** or **Frank fails to find the killer.** You may say to yourself that the second resolution is unacceptable, that you want to write a novel in which the detective succeeds. That's my inclination, too, and I believe that's what most readers want: the triumph of the detective over the villain. But it's certainly possible to write a mystery in which the detective fails at his or her job. Or in which the reader is left wondering if the right person was accused of the crime.

The Spine of the Novel

At this point you might be thinking, "This exercise is

interesting, but it hardly tells me how to develop the plot." The purpose of this exercise is for you to be certain of the basic elements of your plot: what the hero wants, what the obstacle(s) is, and what the outcome is. The first two lines of this three-line statement constitute the spine or through-line of your novel. Everything else about your plot will branch off from this spine.

If you want to write a novel that engages the reader, don't let go of the through-line. Remember it, and remember that the actions in your novel must pertain to it. In police procedurals and private eye novels, writers usually keep the through-line in mind and make sure that the actions are connected to the through-line. It's in amateur detective novels that some authors lose sight of the spine. I've read amateur detective novels in which chapter upon chapter details the hero's life or occupation and connects to the spine only occasionally. In a way that makes sense, because the amateur is not a professional, and solving a murder might not be his/her main want in a novel. Perhaps his or her main want is keeping her job! Or receiving a promotion. Or removing himself from the police's list of suspects. All of these seem realistic wants for an amateur detective. And if one of them is what your amateur detective wants above all, then go with that as the driving element of the plot. Just don't lose sight of it as you develop the plot.

In developing the plot for *Sound Proof* I came up with these three lines as the spine of the novel.

Frank wants to discover who murdered Stubbs
but there are many suspects with equal motives for murder
Frank solves the crime

Let's talk about the number of suspects for a moment. Most mystery writers agree that there should be at least three prime suspects, and probably no more than five or six. In his wonderful book *Writing Crime Fiction*, H.R.F. Keating, author of the Inspector Ghote novels, thought that six was the ideal number of suspects. A number of suspects greater than five or six usually diffuses the tension and somehow lessens the payoff. And a number of suspects fewer than three just isn't interesting: either A or B is pretty cut and dried. But throw in C as an outrider and things become more interesting.

Because the setting of my novel was at a folk festival attended by about 200 people (I wanted that number for authenticity and "feel"), and because Shelby Stubbs insulted just about everybody, I knew there would be a lot of suspects. I tried to confine it to five main suspects, but I can tell from reader comments that many felt there were six or seven suspects. In any case, what was a problem for me (narrowing the suspects down to five) was also a problem for my detective. Out of 200 people, most with motive and means and opportunity, how could he determine who the killer was? I'll deal more with the suspects in a later chapter: I mention it here first because the number of suspects was one of the "but" problems that faced my hero. The other "but" problem turned out to be a motive from the past, although I didn't develop that part of the plot until I got around to the characters and their motivations.

Cause and Effect

There's one other aspect of plot to master in order to write a good mystery. That element is cause-and-effect. In a plot one event causes another. One event doesn't merely follow another, it is *caused* by the previous event. This lends a sense of inevitability to the plot, a marching forward in a logical but perhaps frightening way.

My original notes on the plot for *Sound Proof* went like this:

> **A. Shelby Stubbs insults and thwarts the dreams of just about everybody**
> **B. Stubbs is murdered at the music festival**
> **C. Frank discovers the body and calls the sheriff**
> **D. The sheriff suspects Frank, partly because Frank called in the crime**
> **E. In order to achieve justice and do his job, Frank vows to solve the murder**
> **F. Mary Ployd, festival organizer who hired Frank, warns him off, telling him to leave the murder alone**

G. **There is a second attempt at murder**
H. **Frank solves the crime**

In the bare-bones outline above you can see a cause-and-effect between some (but not all) of the plot points. The cause-and-effect exists between A and B but not between B and C: so I knew that I would have to create a cause for Event C. There's a cause-and-effect between C and D and between D and E, but not between E an F. Again, I knew I would have to create a cause between E and F.

When I first started working out the plot of *Sound Proof* I was hesitant about having a second murder, only because second murders are often so predictable in mystery novels. But I did want to increase the stakes, so I decided that there would be a second *attempt* at murder (Event G). Whether the second murder would be merely attempted or actual, I knew that I would have to create a cause for Event G to occur. As for the connection between all these events and the final one, Event H, I had no idea! Not when I started. I knew that I would have to flesh out these plot points, making sure cause-and-effect existed.

Plot Points

A word about plot points. A plot point is an event in the story. Not just any event, but an event that either moves the plot forward or sends it off in a different direction (which is movement, though not necessarily forward). A plot point can be major or minor: a meaty novel will have both kinds. Plot points serve to raise the stakes of the story, and thus plot points keep reader interest alive and increase tension. Plot points are the vertebrae that make up the spine of the novel.

Before you actually sit down (or stand up, if you prefer) to write your novel, you might want to spend a few months thinking about it. I invariably spend two or three months thinking about the plot, characters, and setting of each novel I write. As you think about plot (and then this happened, and then, and then . . . .) write down each plot point either on a sheet of paper or on a notecard. The notecard method, explained by Robert Kernen in *Building Better*

Plots, is more flexible than the paper or paper-scraps method. Kernen suggests you spread out your notecards (each of which contains only one plot point) on a large table or counter and manipulate them, the better to see which event might logically or cleverly cause another. The manipulation allows you to consider things in a new way, perhaps radically different from what you originally thought. And when it comes to plot, that "radically different from what you originally thought" could be a very good thing.

As long as I'm talking about plot points I want to say that it's usual to place the murder or other crime (each a plot point) near the front of the book. Think of how many times you've picked up a mystery novel and by page one the murder has already occurred. Often. More than often. An already-completed murder or a murder that happens very early in the book immediately sets the detective in motion, makes his or her motives clear, establishes the high ground (murder is a monstrous crime and the criminal must be brought to justice), and gets the reader excited.

When I started *Dirty Proof,* the murder of Ralph Blasingame had already taken place, outside the pages of the novel. The murder and then the police's suspicion of Suzanne Quering, and her coming to Frank Dragovic for help, set the plot in motion.

For *Sound Proof* I wanted a different scenario: I wanted murder victim Shelby Stubbs alive and interacting with people at the beginning of the book. In *Talking About Detective Fiction,* P. D. James indicates that she often prefers that the to-be-murdered person is alive in the first part of the book, so that readers can better understand the reasons why this person was murdered. I wanted Stubbs alive, and I wanted him alive for the whole first day of the festival. He is murdered at night, which means that the murder occurs on about page sixty, at the end of the first day. This gives Frank the remaining four days to solve the crime. Most readers are willing to go along with this pace. Perhaps some of them even anticipate that it's Stubbs who will be killed. (They might even relish the thought of it!) But for some readers, impatient for murder to occur and the game to be afoot, sixty pages is too long to wait.

You will decide for yourself where in your book the murder plot point occurs. I'm a fairly patient reader, but I've put down mysteries in which I reach page 100 and the murder still hasn't occurred. One of the reasons I put them down is that the hero (police, private, or amateur detective) still has no *want* that is her driving force. This lack of a want/desire makes it difficult for me to empathize with the protagonist: she seems to be walking through the novel waiting for something to happen.

Adding Plot Points

Having read thousands of mystery novels, I'm very aware of what I as a reader like and don't like. As I worked on the plotting of *Sound Proof*, I was aware that I might not like a book in which the detective doesn't have a "want" until page sixty. And so I accounted for that in my plotting. What I did, immediately after deciding the bare bones of the plot as outlined earlier, is this: I gave Frank a strong motive for being at Midwest Music Madness in the first place, so that from page one onward he has a driving need.

If I were writing a novel with an amateur detective hero, I would have simply sent Frank to the music festival and have the murder occur and then give Frank some motive for solving the crime. But Frank Dragovic is a professional private eye and I know very well, from knowing his character, that he is not a musician. He listens to music (mostly rock, reggae, and country western), but he has never played an instrument. So, what is he doing at the music festival?

Enter Suzanne Quering from *Dirty Proof*. Frank is in love with Suzanne and wants her to move in with him. Suzanne has not said yes to this proposal. Meanwhile, Suzanne's former babysitter from nearly thirty years ago, Mary Ployd, once a folk singer but now a farm owner and music festival organizer in Iroquois County, Illinois, has asked Suzanne for help. Mary needs help because at each of the two previous Madness old-time music weeks, a stringed instrument was stolen. Mary is afraid that people will stop coming to her festival during old-time week. So she asks Suzanne for help because Mary knows that Suzanne knows a detective.

Suzanne relays this to Frank, and Frank, wanting to please her, agrees to attend Midwest Music Madness undercover, working as a carpenter on the festival grounds. Thus Frank's motives are, indeed, to solve a crime — the crime of instrument theft. He is on the job from page one. And later, after the murder occurs, Frank's "wants" are two: solve the instrument theft and solve the murder.

Here, then, are changes I made to the working outline for *Sound Proof*:

> **A. Frank attends Midwest Music Madness in order to determine who has been stealing instruments and in order to please Suzanne**
> **B. Observing suspects, Frank also observes that Shelby Stubbs insults and thwarts the dreams of just about everybody**
> **C. Stubbs is murdered at the music festival**
> **D. Frank discovers the body and calls the sheriff**
> **E. The sheriff suspects Frank, partly because Frank called in the crime**
> **F. In order to achieve justice and do his job, Frank vows to solve the murder**
> **G. Mary Ployd, festival organizer, warns Frank off, telling him to solve the instrument-theft problem and leave the murder alone**
> **H. There is a second attempt at murder**
> **I. Frank solves the crime**

In the rewritten outline, I've added plot points which more clearly show the cause-and-effect relationship between events. I still haven't solved all the cause-and-effect connections, but this reworked outline is stronger than the first one.

This brief outline served as my starting plot for *Sound Proof*. Frank's wanting to solve both the instrument thefts and later the murder were my through-lines — I tried to make sure that everything Frank did pertained to one of these two wants in every chapter.

Likewise, once you have your basic plot and know your spine or through-line, don't let go of it. Keep it in mind as you write. Think of what motivates your hero, and put that into your writing.

3 Naming Your Characters

You may think it strange that a chapter on naming your characters comes before the chapter on characters themselves. You might ask: don't I need to know who my characters are before I can name them?

The answer is that your character's name is part of who your character is. In most cases, your characters' names are very important parts of who they are. Names connote: they imply or suggest something to the reader. Because connotations are personal as well as cultural, they may differ from reader to reader, but in general the majority of readers will have similar reactions.

The Rhythm of Names

Take, for instance, the name *Harry Potter*. I consider this name absolutely perfect for the author's intentions. In Britain *Harry* is an endearing name in its own right, but it's also used as a familiar name for various King Henry heroes in Shakespeare's plays. The name means *soldier* in Old English and *army ruler* in Scandinavian, both old meanings being good for Rowling's purposes.

The last name *Potter* is a magnificent choice, alluding perhaps to a potter's field where the unclaimed are buried, touching on the commonality of all humans. And just as strong is the association with pottery. Without the invention of pottery and the making of pots by potters, early peoples would not have been able to store water or grains or other foods. In many cultures, pots were necessary to harvest salt. By sealing and thus protecting a tribe's food for the winter, clay pots helped people survive. So the potter was a very, very important contributor to a tribe's survival, growth, and prosperity.

Finally, there's the **TA-dum TA-dum** sound of Harry Potter's name. **HAR-ry POT-ter**. In poetry a **TA-dum** foot is a trochee. The most common stress in the English language is iambic: **ta-DUM** ta-**DUM**. Shakespeare's players are written in iambic pentameter, for example. The trochee is less common, though it's used a lot in children's rhymes, and William Blake used it (**TY**ger **TY**ger **BUR**ning **BRIGHT**). I've always thought the trochee, in small amounts, a very strong and memorable beat — which is another reason why I love the name *Harry Potter*. Many English names are trochee names, but not all of them are two-trochee names. **Jack RY-an** is a one-trochee name and lacks the double-punch of **HAR-ry POT-ter.**

I'm not saying you're required to name your characters in two-syllable trochee names. Rather, I'm saying think about the associations you want readers to have with the names of your characters, and then work hard to come up with a name that meets those impressions and associations.

Katniss Everdeen (she's the protagonist in *The Hunger Games*) is a name I have mixed feelings about. I like the last name because, first, it brings to mind the word *evergreen*, with its connotations not only of vigor and freshness, but also long-lastingness. And the *deen* part of the name suggests *dean*, which means *head*, or *leader*.

But then comes *Katniss*, which I partly like and partly dislike. I like the *Kat* part because the *K* is a strong sound and a pleasing-to-see letter. (Pleasing to me.) But I dislike the name tapering off into an *iss* ending, which is not strong. The name seems to end in weakness or hissing. Or both.

Nor do I like the fact that what comes to mind when seeing the word *katniss* on paper are the words *catnip* or *catnap*. I've had many people tell me that the first thing they think of when reading the hero's name is *catnip*. Later, of course, that association goes away, as one gets to know Katniss and sees her strength. But the initial associations are there, and for me, at least, they linger throughout the trilogy. I'm telling you my personal reactions to this name so that you can see how a reader might react to your characters' names.

She's on First, a baseball story, was my very first published novel. I named the protagonist *Linda Sunshine*. In terms of beat, that's **LIN**da **SUN**shine. Two trochee feet, just like *Harry Potter* (who wasn't around back when I wrote *She's on First*). So there is something about the trochee that appeals to me. I chose the last name *Sunshine* because it's a compound word and a life-affirming word: without the rays of the sun, there would be no life on Earth. I chose *Linda* as my hero's first name both because it's a common name and because it's a simple name. The name means *beautiful*, but that didn't factor into my decision.

When it came to naming my detective hero, I knew immediately that his first name would be *Frank*, even though that's not as common a first name as it once used to be. Growing up, I knew many Croatian men named Frank. The name is of German or Teutonic origin, and it means *free*. A private eye must certainly be free to operate as he or she pleases, to follow the truth wherever it leads him. Plus, in English the word *frank* means *open, honest, direct, sincere* — definitely the character traits of my protagonist.

For the last name I wanted a name of Croatian origins. I chose Dragovic, which in Croatian and Serbian means *son of beloved*. In Serbo-Croatian *drago* meaning *beloved*. But in Italian it means *dragon*. The name is not pronounced **DRAG**, but rather **DRAHG**. (Frank has something to say about the pronunciation of his name in *Dirty Proof*.) So in rhythm, the name is **FRANK DRAHG-o-vic**. The single-beat first name and the dactylic (a three-beat measure with stress on the first beat) last name make for a strong sounding name. Dactyls were the primary beat of epic Latin poetry. Henry Wadsworth Longfellow used dactyls for "Evangeline." And the Beatles song, "Lucy in the Sky with Diamonds" is written in dactyls. For me, the name and the beat worked to connote an honest, reliable character.

Changing Names

I said earlier that it helps to know your characters by name before you start developing them in other ways (age, education, work skills, love interests, family, plus character traits and personality traits). This doesn't mean you have to name each character before you begin writing, or even before you begin developing aspects of that character. In writing *Sound Proof*, for example, I had the names of Frank Dragovic and Suzanne Quering from *Dirty Proof*, and I chose the name for Mary Ployd, the festival organizer, before

I began developing her. For many of the other characters I actually chose which instrument they played before I chose their names. But I did choose their names early in the process of developing them: not the first thing about them, but near the front of the list.

As I worked on the novel I changed some names. You will most likely do that, too. In *Sound Proof* I astonished myself by changing a name the day before publication! In all but the final draft of the book, the Sheriff was named *Yancey Davis*. However, one of the suspects is named *Vance Jurasek*. All along I had been harboring subconscious concern about these two similar (too-similar!) sounding names, *Yancey* and *Vance*, and I feared readers might mix them up. Readers often express confusion over similar-sounding character names. So at the last minute, before it was too late, I did a Search/Find/Change function on my computer and *Yancey Davis* became *Yale Davis*.

After I did that, I thought: *Yale. Lock. Sheriff. Duh!* Why I didn't come up with the name *Yale* from the beginning, I have no idea. But this goes to show that our subconscious is always at work, critiquing our decisions, prodding us to make better ones. It's often very wise to listen to your self-conscious. It certainly was in this case.

Starting Letters

This Yancey-to-Yale switch brings up another aspect of naming characters, and that's the letters that start their names. Many readers (and I have been one of them) get confused when too many (sometimes just two!) character names start with the same letter of the alphabet. I made this mistake when writing *Dirty Proof,* and I wish I could undo it. But I can't, because the characters I named are continuing characters.

First I started with the name *Suzanne Quering,* Frank's client in *Dirty Proof.* I like the name *Suzanne*: it's a strong name. It's not as common as *Susan,* and I liked that. The z is ever-so-mildly exotic. The double-n is strong. The name means *graceful lily,* and Suzanne is lithe and an acrobat. In the *Book of Daniel* Suzanne is falsely accused by two elders. Rather than succumb to their blackmail, she defends herself. The name *Suzanne* connotes a strong person. Did I know all of this when I chose the name? No, but I felt some of it, and as I developed the character, the name helped me. It is, as I said, good to name your main characters before you begin developing them — keeping in mind that you can always change the names, first and/or last, if your character becomes a different person, one whom your original name no longer suits.

For Frank's sister, a minor character in the book, but somebody he mentions frequently, I went through a whole gamut of names and came up with *Stefani*. This was a common name for Croatian-American girls when I was growing up. In addition, I thought that the two names together, *Frank* and *Stefani*, sounded like a brother and sister: definitely a Croatian-American brother and sister.

Right then and there, in choosing the name *Stefani*, I should have heeded the advice about not starting the names of two different characters with the same letter.

Not only didn't I heed the advice, I did something worse. For a minor character, a fellow private eye Frank sometimes works with, I chose the name *Sarah Bellam*, which is nothing more than a play on the word *cerebellum*. So now I had three female characters, one major and two minor, whose names started with the letter *S*. Readers find that confusing. And when I said I couldn't change this, I meant it. Frank's sister is mentioned in *Sound Proof* and will be in other novels. Sarah Bellam won't appear in every *Proof* novel, but she will appear in some. So I messed up on this. You can learn from my mistakes and not do the same thing.

Aware that I had messed up a set of name choices in *Dirty Proof*, I vowed to make better character-naming decisions in *Sound Proof*. Creating an alphabet sheet, I began to mark the letters of the alphabet, using circles if a character's first name began with that letter, rectangles if a character's last name began with that letter.

Would that I had thought of such a chart when writing *Dirty Proof*. But except for my mistake with the *S* names, I'm not sure I needed a chart: there aren't that many characters in *Dirty Proof*.

With *Sound Proof*, however, I faced the problem of having many, many characters. Remember that there are approximately

200 people attending a week-long music festival. I didn't need names for even half that amount: that would be overwhelming. But I did need names for the festival organizer and her assistant, for the five main suspects, for a few of the teachers and a few of the vendors, and for a few of the cooks. Plus the sheriff. All told, I probably needed twenty-five names. That's why this alphabet chart was so important to me.

As you can see on the chart, in a few cases I had more than one character sharing the same letter of the alphabet. There's *Dragovic, Davis* (the sheriff) and *Dufour* (the hammered dulcimer player). They're all men, too, whereas the two G names, *Grayson* and *Glover*, are respectively a woman and a man, and the two S

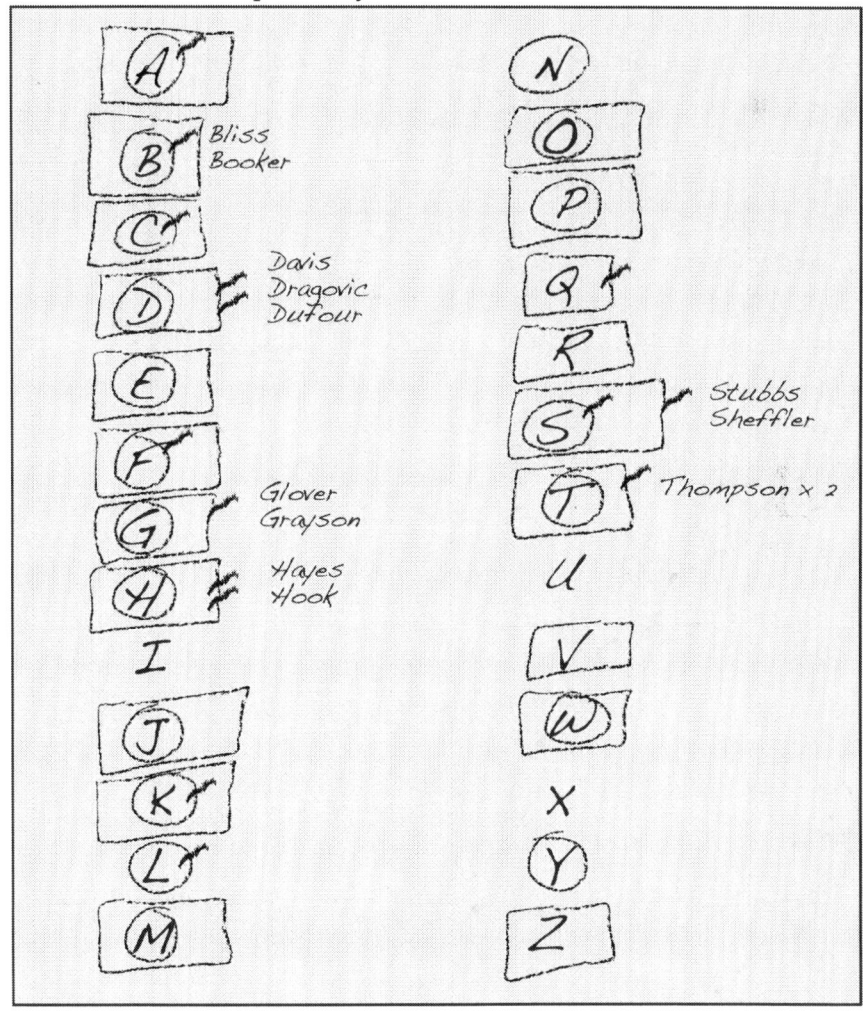

A	
B	Bliss, Booker
C	
D	Davis, Dragovic, Dufour
E	
F	
G	Glover, Grayson
H	Hayes, Hook
I	
J	
K	
L	
M	
N	
O	
P	
Q	
R	
S	Stubbs, Sheffler
T	Thompson × 2
U	
V	
W	
X	
Y	
Z	

names, *Stubbs* and *Sheffler*, are a man and a woman.

I decided that I could go with *Davis* as the last name of the sheriff because he would usually be called *Sheriff*, or *Sheriff Yale Davis*, so that was no problem. Seldom, if ever, would I call him just *Davis*. As to *Dufour*, he would be called by his first name, *Guy*, and occasionally by both names.

Maybe this means that despite my own advice, and despite the advice of many writers, I have a proclivity for naming characters with the same letter of the alphabet. I don't know. But I offer it as something you can consider when choosing your character names. If you're going to have characters whose names start with the same letter, don't make the mistake I did in *Dirty Proof*: having three women all roughly the same age, all their first names starting with S. In *Sound Proof* I was at least aware of the fact that I was using the same letter for certain names, and I figured out how I could make that less confusing.

Ethnic Names

Finally, when choosing names for your characters, remember that the United States is a nation of many, many different nationalities. Even though the thirty most common last names in the 2010 US census are all either Anglo-Saxon — (*Davis*, for instance, is the seventh most common last name in the US, *Smith* being the most common); Latino (*Garcia* is the eighth most common last name, and *Rodriguez* the ninth); or Asian (*Lee* is the twenty-second most common last name) — this top-thirty breakdown represents European-Americans, African-Americans, Spanish-Americans, and Asian-Americans.

Up until fairly recently, say the early 1980s, character names in American mystery writing were usually Anglo-Saxon last names. Charlie Chan, created by Earl Derr Biggers in the 1920s, was an exception. Nero Wolfe, created by Rex Stout, was actually from Macedonia (then part of Yugoslavia), but had Anglicized his name. Starting in the late 1950s Chester Hines wrote about African-American police detectives Coffin Ed Johnson and Gravedigger Jones.

Then along came writers such as Sara Paretsky, whose hero is named V.I. Warshawski. Tony Hillerman created Navajos Joe Leaphorn and Jimmy Chee. Today, more than thirty years later, mystery novels in the US are populated with detectives from a host of different ethnic backgrounds. This introduction of more representative (i.e., not pure Anglo-Saxon) characters and names into detective literature was a breath of fresh air, reflecting life as most of us know it. When you start to decide on names for your characters, think about the ethnicity of the people you know in your workplace. Think about the last names of your children's friends.

Pick up a telephone book (at a local library or historical society) that represents the kind of area you're writing about and browse through the names. If, however, you're writing about a pocket of the country that is almost all Anglo-Saxon in heritage, then your names will reflect that. It might be artificial to introduce other ethnic names. But chances are that the telephone book (or on-line directory) you consult will reflect a wide variety of names. Consider some of those last names, possibly slightly altered, as names for your characters.

Books on Name Origins

When I teach writing fiction, I always talk about naming characters, and I bring with me two books on American last names. Unfortunately, both of these books are out of print. But you may find one or both at your local library. If not, you can request that your library get the book for you through InterLibrary Loan.

The first of these books is *Family Names: The Origins, Meanings, Mutations, and History of More than 2,800 American Names*, by J. N. Hook, , published in 1983 by Collier Books. This book consists of thirty-five chapters which look at the waves of immigration for different ethnic groups. Listed are the names of the first immigrants of each group to enter what is today the United States. For example, if I were to look up Croatians, I would find them in the chapter on Southern Slavs and I would learn that many of them immigrated to Louisiana in the late 1700s and early 1800s, and that these immigrants sided with the Confederates during the Civil War. A Confederate solder named George Petrovich, for example, was killed at Gettysburg. This kind of information is invaluable to a writer seeking to name characters.

The second of the books you could consult is *New Dictionary of American Family Names,* by Elsdon C. Smith, published in 1988 by Harper& Row. This book lists, in alphabetical order, more than 25,000 common surnames in the US and gives their nationality or country of origin as well as their meaning. This book is not only out of print, it is outdated in that after it was published far larger numbers of people from Asia, the Mideast, and Africa immigrated here. Their last names are not represented in this book.

As an example of how this second book works, I'll look up my own last name, *Gregorich.* Here's the entry: **Gregorich (Yu.-Sl.) The son of Gregor, Yugoslavian form of Gregory (watchful).**

One of the characters in *Sound Proof* is Lafayette Wafer, and I got his last name directly from the *New Dictionary of American Family Names.* Here's the entry: **Wafer (Eng.) Metonymic for the maker or seller of thin, crisp cakes. They often sold their wares from house to house.** *Metonymic* indicates that the name for the cake (wafer) soon became the name for the person making or selling the thin, crisp cakes.

In creating my characters I search for last names that seem to suit the characters the way I imagine them. And remember: sometimes I change their names because their character changes as I develop it.

Often I find that students want to spend hours and hours with these two books, looking up their own last names, the maiden names of their mothers, the names of their grandparents, the names of their friends, and, last but not least, the names they are considering for their characters. In fact, when I'm on the "naming your characters" part of teaching I usually stay an hour after each class just so students can share these two books (which I bring to class with me, and which I will not leave behind because they are so valuable to me). Often this interest in character names spills over into another day or two, and I bring the books with me and stay overtime again, just so that every student who wants to peruse these books can. I think this indicates how important names are to people: their own real names, and the names of their characters.

First Names

First names are as important as last names, and countless name-your-baby books and online sites purport to tell you the meaning of every possible baby name. Your problem in choosing a first name for your character is that the choices seem endless: not only are there names such as *John* and *Mary* which have been around Europe and Russia and South America for centuries (in various forms such as *Ian, Johann, Owen,* or *Marie, Mae, Maika,* or *Manette*), there are more modern names whose popularity comes and goes by decade or century: names such as *Scott* and *Jennifer*, for example, or *Ashley* and *Jacob*.

Speaking of first names, let me digress for a moment to say that you can look up first names of men and women by decade through the US Census Bureau website. If you want to write about a character who is now 40 years old, figure out which decade she was born in and go to the Census Bureau site to look up the most popular baby names for that decade. You can choose one of those popular names for your characters. Unless, of course, you want her to have a not-so-common first name for that decade.

In certain parts of the country and in certain cultures it has always been popular to give a child the last name of the mother, or the last name of the grandmother in order to keep that last name in the family. Thus you can have children whose first names are *Taylor, Parker, Carter, Jackson, Madison,* and so on. Today this trend is popular in another way: giving children "power" names. That is, naming them after institutions or enterprises or concepts. *Chase* is a common first name right now . . . maybe named after Chase Bank?

In *Sound Proof,* having more characters than usual, I also of course had more names to decide on.

Here are some of the names I came up with.

Characters in *Sound Proof*
Protagonist
Frank Dragovic — Chicago private detective. The last name is Croatian. (It can also be Serbian.)

Festival Personnel

Mary Ployd — folk singer, organizer of Midwest Music Madness. The last name is Welsh. I chose *Ployd*, the less usual version of *Floyd*.

Nola Grayson — Mary's attorney, conference go-to person. The last name is English, and I chose it because of the folk song "Tom Dooley," in which Grayson foils Tom Dooley. I chose *Nola* because it's not common. Its origins are both Irish and Italian.

Teachers

Shelby Stubbs — legendary old-time fiddler and murder victim. I chose *Shelby* because it's a common last name in the South. Stubbs is from the South, as are many old-time musicians, both in real life and in my novel. I chose *Stubbs* because a stub is the truncated remains of something: a cigarette, a ticket, etc. I associated this with Stubbs trampling on and thus truncating people's dreams.

Raven Hook — autoharp player, Shelby's ex-wife. I chose the name *Raven* partly because it sounded folky to me, but mainly because ravens are keen-eyed, intelligent, and may steal things. Raven has become bitter, and I thought the last name *Hook* suited her: hooks are sharp and can hurt.

Kofi Quay — African drummer, from Ghana. I looked up African names from that country and chose these.

Bliss Beckins — Shelby's current wife. I chose the first name because in addition to connoting euphoria, it suggests a kind of obliviousness. I think I made up the last name.

Edric English — guitar player in Shelby's band, also from the South. The last name is English (surprise!). So is the first name.

Booker Hayes — guitar player. Booker is African-American, and I chose his first name from Booker T. Washington, his last from common African-American surnames.

Students

Suzanne Quering — Frank Dragovic's lover. I've already mentioned how I chose Suzanne's first name. I wanted her last name to begin with a *Q*, because few do, so I knew this would make it easier for the reader to remember her. I don't know how or where I came up with the last name, but I wanted it to sound Scandinavian.

Guy Dufour — hammered dulcimer player, also plays hurdy-gurdy and bones. Guy is from Maine, which is in part ethnically French (from Quebec), so I wanted both of his names to be French.

Cindy Ruffo — mountain dulcimer player. Her first name comes from the folk song, "Get Along Home Little Cindy." Her last name is Italian in origin.

Fonnie Sheffler — guitar and autoharp player. I made up the first name. That is to say, I didn't find it in any baby-naming book, but I'll bet there's somebody out there named *Fonnie*. I think men named *Alfonso* might be called *Fonnie*, but my character is a woman. Who knows, maybe she was named *Alphonsa* or such and uses the nickname. Or perhaps it's her given first name. I don't know: but I do know that I wanted an unusual first name, one that suggested falseness. *Fonnie* is something like *Phoney*, so I went with it. I don't even remember how I came up with it. The last name, *Sheffler*, is German.

Cody Thompson — eleven years old, son of Tansy Thompson. Cody is a popular boy's first name, so I went with that. The origins of *Thompson* are Anglo-Saxon.

Vance Jurasek — mandolin player. The first name comes from the Credence Clearwater Revival song, "Vance Can't Dance," and the last name is Czech and Slovak. Vance is from the Midwest, where a Czech or Slovak last name would be somewhat common.

Lafayette Wafer — bowed psaltry player. Lafayette is from Louisiana, and Lafayette is a town in Louisiana named after Lafayette, the French general who aided Washington and the Patriots during the American Revolution, and whose help played such an important role in the winning of the war. The name suggests strength and loyalty. But the character Lafayette is thin, reedy, and perhaps not reliable, so I wanted his first name and his last name to be at odds. Because he's so thin, I came up with the name *Wafer*, which is English in origin and suggests not only thinness but also insubstantiality.

Vendors

Jeff Glover — sells fiddles, bones, autoharps, and other instruments.

One of the meanings of *Jeff* is *traveler*, and the character Jeff comes to the Illinois festival from far away: Wyoming. *Jeff* also means *peaceful gift*. His last name is English. A glove covers or conceals. As with the name Lafayette Wafer, I wanted the two parts of Jeff Glover's names to be at war with one another, indicating that the reader doesn't really know Jeff. (Or Lafayette.)

Kim Oberfeld — sells fiddles, autoharps, guitars. She's from Milwaukee, a town settled largely by German-Americans, so I gave her a German last name. I'm not sure why I chose the first name: possibly because it's so different from the other female names that I felt it would help the reader remember who Kim was.

Aurora Townspeople

Aja Freeman — a cook at Midwest Music Madness. *Aja* is not that unusual a first-name, especially for young African-American women. I've encountered several *Aja's* in the last ten years. At least one of them was named after Steely Dan's best-selling album. *Freeman* is a common African-American last name.

Tansy Thompson — a cook at Midwest Music Madness, mother of Cody Thompson. I chose the first name because it sounded small-town to me, a name that might be passed down generation to generation. A tansy is a flower. *Tansy* can be Latin, Greek, or Native American: it's used in all these cultures.

Yale Davis — sheriff of Aurora. Both the first name and the last name are English and/or Welsh. I've already explained that this character's name throughout all but the last version of *Sound Proof* was *Yancey*, and why I changed that, and what a fortunate change it turned out to be.

All of this thinking about names might look like a lot of work to you, and you might think you can avoid it. Well, yes, you can avoid it — but then the names of your characters won't be as deep or meaningful, or interest readers as much, as if you gave this some thought. And it's not as difficult as it looks. In addition to the non-accountable time (while cooking, exercising, showering, and so on) that I spent thinking about character names, I spent approximately 45 minutes per name with a name book. Considering how important names are, that's not a lot of time. Furthermore, it's fun time, thinking of what to name people and learning about names as you browse through one of the two books I mentioned.

In conclusion, I'll repeat what I started out with in this chapter: it's very helpful to a writer to start naming his characters before he gets to know them fully. Naming a character gives you a sense of accomplishment and allows you to think of the character as an actual person.

4 Developing Major Characters

In addition to your protagonist you might have one other major character who is not a suspect. As discussed earlier, this other major character could act as an antagonist (not the villain), a mirror, and/or a romance. In addition to that you need at least three suspects, but usually no more than six. Of your suspects, all can be major characters, or some can be major and some can be minor. In this chapter, though, I will deal only with major characters.

Your hero, of course, is one of your major characters, and all aspects of character development apply to him or her.

The first thing you need to know about your hero is that she or he should not be you. The risk in modeling your hero after yourself is that you will not pay much attention to what the character's motivation is, what her or his actions are, and why. You won't pay much attention because your protagonist will be so much *you* that you will simply write what you would do, without analyzing it. This will weaken your character because you won't have taken much care or given much thought to *building* the character.

Your characters are not you. They are created by you, but they have a life of their own. They proceed according to the logic of their story. This doesn't mean that parts of you aren't in the characters you create. They definitely are — in *all* the characters you create, heroes and villains. But these story people contain selected parts of your character and personality, not the entirety of who you are.

Borrowing Real-Life Characters

And what about your friends (or your enemies) — is it wise to model your characters on them? You've probably read about cases in which authors are sued by somebody who feels defamed because (they say) a character in the author's book is "clearly" modeled on them. Sometimes the suers win, sometimes they don't. Often the case is dismissed, or settled out of court. When the suer loses, it's most often because there are too many differences between the real-life person and the book character: differences in appearance, age, sex, education, nationality, and occupation.

What strikes me in reading about these cases, though, is how often there are many similarities between the real-life person and the character in the book. Their names might be very similar, even sharing the same initials. Their occupation might be the same. They might be physically similar. For example, Kathryn Stockett, author of *The Help,* was sued by Ablene Cooper, an African-American nanny who claimed that the character of Aibileen Clark, African-American nanny, was modeled on her. (Cooper's case was dismissed because the one-year statute of limitations had elapsed.)

No writer I know of wants to be sued over their creations. There are ways to help avoid lawsuits. Back when I began writing fiction, I read scores of books on the subject, and one piece of advice I picked up is this: if you're going to borrow the character traits of people you know, then proceed as follows.

For each character you create, borrow traits from *at least three different people* you know, not *one* person you know. Let's say, for example, that you want to create a character named Jacquie Boyle. To help characterize her, you have her wear dark-colored flower-print dresses, just like Janis, the friend of one of your friends, wears. *Oops!* Right there, it's best to change Jacquie's first name because it starts with the same first letter as does *Janis*. Okay, so you change her first name to something less common than *Jacquie* or *Janis* . . . *Portia*, say, or something you make up, like *Pelé*. So the name is now *Pelé Boyle*.

Next, you give Pelé an autistic child who needs special care, which requires a lot of money and which places Pelé under great stress. You borrow the autistic-child situation from somebody you've never met but hear about often because she's the first cousin of the man who cuts your hair. That mother, whom you hear about from your hairdresser each month, is named Lucia Bogatta. *Oops!* Her last name starts with the same initial as does Pelé Boyle's. To be safe, you change your character's last name to *Grady*. Notice that *Bogatta* and *Grady* are not the same nationality: the first is Italian, the second is Irish. *Good!* Pelé Grady is looking less and less like any one person.

Then, still thinking about your mystery and its characters, you remember somebody who used to work for the same company you still work for. Her initials were not *PG*, and she wasn't Irish. You remember her because five years earlier she embezzled a quarter of a million dollars from the company before she was caught in a yearly audit. So now you have your character Pelé Grady, who dresses in dark-colored flower-print dresses, has an autistic child, and is embezzling money from the company she works for.

That is step one. If you feel you must borrow from people you really know, borrow from at least three different people to create one character. But then go further. You can change the nationality of your character so that it matches none of the characters you borrowed from. You can also change the age: from a 30-year-old to a 55-year-old, for example. Or from a 55-year-old to a teen. You can and *should* change the character's occupation so that it's radically different from those of the real-life people you borrowed from. And you can change the sex. *Pelé Grady* can become *Porto Grundy*.

Remember that what you're interested in is *who* your character is and what motivates him or her. You are *not*, or should not be, interested in creating characters similar to people you know. That way lies possible damage.

External Characteristics

When it comes to creating major characters, you need to know the external and the internal. The external includes your character's height, weight, hair color, eye color, the type of clothing he or she wears, any unusual physical traits (walks with a limp, for example), the sound of his or her voice, body odor (if any!), gait (light? heavy?), and so on.

Some writers actually take weeks or months of their writing time to create physical-description charts for each of their main (and sometimes minor) characters, often including the characters's date of birth, the names of his parents and siblings, where he went to school, and his Zodiac sign. Me, I doodle on bits of paper until I figure out what my characters look like, then I type up a brief description.

Here are a few examples from *Sound Proof.*

Frank Dragovic — 30 years old; 6 feet tall; 172 pounds; brown hair; brown eyes

Suzanne Quering — 28 years old; tall; lithe; gray eyes; red hair, worn long

Mary Ployd — in her 60s; large-boned, sturdy; graying brown hair worn in a long braid

Booker Hayes — late 40s; African-American; tall; muscular

Raven Hook — late 40s; thin; long black hair; melodious singing voice

Lafayette Wafer — mid-50s; 5'8" tall; very thin; gray hair; wispy gray beard; reedy voice

The purpose of these brief physical descriptions is mainly for me, the writer, so that I can imagine what the characters look like as they're interacting. Also, I like to convey something of what the character looks like to the reader, so that the reader, too, can "see" the characters. I don't convey this all at once, as I've done in the examples above. Instead, I introduce a character's looks bit by bit in some cases, all at once in others. As a reader, I like it when a writer helps me see his characters more than once. That is, I dislike "information dumps" the first time I meet a character.

As I began to write *Sound Proof,* I further developed the physical characteristics of each character as I wrote about the person in action. Mary Ployd, for example, tends to not *walk* to where she's going, but *march* to where she's going. She is determined and full of purpose. Mary is also authoritative and believes that when she declares something is so, it *is* so. To indicate this, I gave her the gesture of placing her hands in front of herself, palms downward, and then sweeping her arms out to the side — as if to indicate, "And that's final!" I used both her marching stride and her hand gesture several times throughout the novel.

Lafayette dresses in a disheveled manner. He carries his bowed psaltry with him wherever he goes. When somebody is speaking to him, Lafayette is as apt to play a tune on the psaltry as he is to answer. After he has quaffed quantities of cheap alcohol, he appears to not be following the conversation. Again, as with Mary

Ployd, I interspersed these physical characteristics of Lafayette's throughout the book. Such physical descriptions help characterize, so that a reader is better able to imagine and relate to your fictional creations.

External characteristics are of course a small part of the big picture of who your characters are, just as in real life the way people look tells you only a bit about what they're like. Physical characteristics are not the main part of who a person is. We are a combination of our external selves, our internal selves, and our actions. When creating characters, allow yourself to think hard about all of these.

Personality

Internal characteristics can be divided into personality and character, and the best writers understand both. Understanding the distinction between *personality* and *character* helps you create believable characters in your writing. There's an excellent explanation of the difference between the two in an article that Alex Lickerman. M.D., wrote for *Psychology Today*. The article was published on April 3, 2011 and is available online.

Dr. Lickerman explains that personality is what we first see when we engage with another person: "We judge people funny, extroverted, energetic, optimistic, confident — as well as overly serious, lazy, negative, and shy — if not upon first meeting them, then shortly thereafter." Think of all the personalities Dr. Lickerman has listed in just this one sentence: you can use them to create the personalities (but *not* the characters) of your fictional people.

To give you an example, here are the personalities of the same characters I listed above.

> **Frank Dragovic** — 30 years old; 6 feet tall; 172 pounds; brown hair; brown eyes.
> Confident. Energetic. Patient.
> **Suzanne Quering** — 28 years old; tall; lithe; gray eyes; red hair, worn long.
> Funny. Energetic.

Mary Ployd — mid-60s; large-boned, sturdy; graying brown hair worn in a long braid.
Confident. Impatient. Forceful.
Booker Hayes — late 40s; African-American; tall; muscular.
Friendly. Reticent.
Raven Hook — late 40s; thin; long black hair; melodious singing voice.
Flirtatious. Negative.
Lafayette Wafer — mid-50s; 5'8" tall; very thin; gray hair; wispy gray beard; reedy voice.
Unconfident. Unfocused. Shy.

According to Dr. Lickerman, people form opinions of others on the basis of personality fairly quickly. But when it comes to character, that takes a much longer time to figure out. Character is deeper. It's not on the surface. Dr. Lickerman states that character traits (honesty or dishonesty, for example, or meanness or kindness) are based on deep-seated beliefs and reveal themselves only in specific circumstances. In other words, character traits, unlike personality traits, are not on the surface.

In real life as well as in fiction, most people pay far more attention to personality than to character. Many people think only of the personality of their friends and acquaintances, not of their character. Psychologists know that as a rule we associate certain personality types with certain character. For example, we tend to assume that an outgoing, funny, gregarious person is kind, generous, and ethical. We might assume that a dour, laconic introvert is stingy, cold-hearted, and untrustworthy. It's easy to form almost-immediate opinions about people based on their personality, which is visible in their body language, facial expressions, and voice. But, until circumstances force us to do so (often ruefully), most of us tend to ignore a person's character.

Character

Despite the fact that most people in real life behave this

way (that is, they judge on personality, not on character), you as a writer need to be deeply aware of both qualities, because you need to know not only the personality of your fictional characters, but, even more importantly, you need to know their character.

Here are the same examples from *Sound Proof,* this time with character added.

Frank Dragovic —
    Physical — 30 years old; 6 feet tall; 172 pounds; brown hair; brown eyes.
    Personality — Confident. Energetic. Patient.
    Character — Trustworthy. Competent. Observant. Just.

Suzanne Quering —
    Physical — 28 years old; tall; lithe; gray eyes; red hair, worn long.
    Personality — Funny. Energetic.
    Character — Kind. Generous. Truthful.

Mary Ployd —
    Physical — mid-60s; large-boned, sturdy; graying hair worn in a long braid.
    Personality — Confident. Impatient. Forceful.
    Character — Manipulative. Penny-Pinching. Ashamed.

Booker Hayes —
    Physical — late 40s; African-American; tall; muscular.
    Personality — Friendly. Reticent.
    Character — Loyal. Trustworthy.

Raven Hook —
    Physical — late 40s; thin; long black hair; melodious singing voice.
    Personality — Flirtatious. Negative.
    Character — Jealous. Vindictive. Untrustworthy.

Lafayette Wafer —
    Physical — mid-50s; 5'8" tall; very thin; gray hair; wispy gray beard; reedy voice.
    Personality — Unconfident. Unfocused. Shy.
    Character — Naive. Generous.

As you develop your fictional characters and write about them, you may find that you want a character's personality to match her inner character. That is, one of your characters (let's name her Kortney Avarkian), who is friendly and easy to laugh, happens to be kind, generous, and trustworthy. And all your other fictional characters assume the same thing about Kortney: her inside matches her outside. There's nothing wrong with proceeding this way in building characters. It's common to assume these things in real life, and it's common to assume them in fiction. But it's also possible for you as a writer to go against type. That is, to have your fictional person's personality be at odds with what most would think about his character.

Writers create better stories when they're aware of character, which runs far deeper than personality. It is character, not personality, that will determine how your fictional people behave in a crunch. It is character that will determine who the killer is and why he kills. So during the time you get to know your fictional characters on all three levels (appearance, personality, and character), think about these things.

One thing's for certain: your detective hero, particularly if a cop or private eye, will understand what character is. He will be able to see into a person through that person's behavior. And he will draw conclusions from a person's behavior. Dr. Lickerman puts it this way: ". . . if we observe someone lie easily, we can be reasonably certain from even just one instance that they've done so in the past and will do so again in the future, as the best predictor of future behavior is past behavior."

Character Motivation

Finally, in developing fictional character, it helps to know what motivates your major characters: what drives these characters to behave the way they do, in the situation they are in. In developing motives for your main characters, you may find that each has more than one motive, depending on the situation.

Here's an example from *Sound Proof*.

Frank Dragovic — He is motivated to help Mary solve the stolen-instruments situation because Suzanne, his lover, asked him to do so. Once on the job, he is always motivated to do a good job. After he is falsely accused by the sheriff, Frank is motivated to prove the sheriff wrong.

Mary Ployd — Mary's motives are complex. She wants to keep her music festival solvent, because if she can't do that she might lose the farm she purchased. She genuinely wants people to have a good time, to enjoy the musical experience, and she knows they can't enjoy themselves if they feel they can't trust their fellow musicians. Mary is motivated by money: she needs it and as a result does things she's ashamed of. Mary has a sense of her own superiority and is motivated to show others that she can do things better than they can.

In an earlier chapter I mentioned that students love the two books on last names that I take to class when teaching fiction. They also love the books I bring on creating characters. There are many, many such books out there, but I usually bring only two of them to class.

The first of these is *The Writer's Guide to Character Traits*, by Linda N. Edelstein, Ph.D, who, at the time she wrote the book, was a practicing psychologist at the Chicago School of Professional Psychology. Dr. Edelstein provides more than four hundred lists that describe personality traits, many of them criminal traits.

The Writer's Guide to Character Traits gives very instructive and helpful explanations of a person's "inside" behavior. I consult this book every time I'm writing a novel. However: I consult it *after*, not before, I've developed my characters. My fear is that using lists and explanations like the one in this book, I might create predictable, stereotyped characters. That's why I like to create my character first, by the methods I've explained, and then use *The Writer's Guide to Character Traits* to perhaps intensify aspects of my characters, or to bring in a plausible unconsidered side of my character.

The other book that I take to class with me is *45 Master Characters: Mythic Models for Creating Original Characters*, by Victoria Lynn Schmidt, who is a screenwriter. Schmidt groups characters into heroes and villains, male and female. That is, she has a section on female heroes and villains, and a section on male heroes and villains. She also has a section on supporting characters (who are neither the heroes nor the villains). Within each section she identifies the hero or villain by archetype, such as Aphrodite, Athena, Hera, or Isis. Or Apollo, Hermes, or Zeus, for example. She proceeds to explore all sides of each archetype.

Schmidt also asks and answers the kinds of questions that writers ask and answer. In the chapter on Aphrodite, for example, subtitled "The Seductive Muse and the Femme Fatale," Schmidt asks the question, *What does the seductive muse care about?* and then proceeds to enumerate these things and discuss them. Schmidt also asks, *What motivates the seductive muse?* And, *How do others see the seductive muse?* Each chapter is set up in this way. These explorations of archetypes and what motivates them, what they crave, what they fear, are excellent aids in helping a writer develop characters.

Characters from the Subconscious

This chapter has shown you how to start creating and developing major characters. But sometimes as you're writing a character just appears on the page, out of nowhere, and you find yourself wondering, *Whoa! Where did he come from?*

Well, the fact is that when you're writing a novel, you're creating a whole new world, and that world begins to reside in your subconscious, which is at work day and night to help you solve any problems you may be having with the book — even if you're unaware that you're having problems with the book. My subconscious doesn't, to my awareness (but then, one is not aware of the subconscious!), intervene in every book. But it does intervene in most books. It has given me names for characters I had a hard time naming: I wake up with the name in mind. And the name fits. It has provided me with the titles of books I was having a hard time titling. And, in the case of *Sound Proof*, my subconscious provided me with one of the characters: Richard.

Richard has only one name. That's because he's a pig. A 600-pound Yorkshire. Mary Ployd's pet. I did not plan Richard. I certainly didn't make a character chart for him! Nor did I consult books on how to develop pigs as characters.

No, Richard came from my subconscious, possibly because I spent much of my childhood on a dairy farm that also had pigs, and one of my jobs was slopping the hogs. Or possibly because my subconscious sensed that with two hundred humans coming and going at an old-time music festival, many of these people playing instruments the average person hasn't heard of and can't imagine (bowed psaltry, hammered dulcimer, bones, spoons, and the like), readers needed somebody they could identify immediately. That somebody being a pig.

There I was, sitting at my computer, composing a summary in which Frank (still undercover as a carpenter) is checking the festival grounds for places where a thief might hide a musical instrument. The day is very hot. Frank has checked the barn, the outbuildings, and the campgrounds, and is now approaching the farmhouse where Mary lives and where certain of the instructors are housed.

Here's what I typed:

> The thermometer on the back stoop read 92°.
> Directly under the thermometer, leaning up against the house siding, a nylon instrument case stood unprotected.
> I couldn't tell by looking what instrument it housed because the case was long, wedge-shaped and blue — like a Cheesehead after a Green Bay winter.
> Lifting the wedge I unzipped it. Inside was a guitar, Tippin by name. A brand I'd never heard of, but I wasn't a musician. Rosewood sides and back, spruce top. Tortoise-shell inlay under the sound hole. Beautiful construction. Worth a few thousand for sure. What was it doing out on the porch in the sizzling heat, at a festival where a thief supposedly picked instruments with the same ease he picked notes? Zipping the case closed, I leaned it against the siding.

And then, out of my subconscious, came the following lines:

> A loud grunt made me jump.
> I turned and found myself facing a pig.
> A five- or six-hundred pound one. Yorkshire, by the looks of it: a white pig with a pinkish hue. Its little

eyes looked at me. Its wet snout quivered. Its bristles looked hoary in the sunlight.

Where did *that* come from, I wondered. How did a pig enter my novel? I thought about it for a minute or two, then decided to go with it. I continued:

> Pigs, my Uncle Rudy always lectured, are not dirty animals. Provided with adequate space, clean bedding, and good eating conditions, pigs remain clean. Except in hot weather. Cursed with inefficient sweat glands, pigs cool themselves in water or mud. The pig confronting me looked as if it had been cooling itself a long time, probably down by the creek. Snorting, it jumped sideways and thundered off in the direction of the old tractor shed, its corkscrew tail bouncing.

That was all for the pig in the above summary from chapter three. But a 600-pound pig is bound to make its presence known. This came later in the same chapter.

> Mary marched toward the vendor area.
> Toward me, to be exact.
> "Frank! Richard has escaped again. You've got to do something."
> *Richard?*
> "Who's Richard?"
> "My pig. Come with me," she commanded, marching off toward the pigpen.
> A porch bell clanged loudly to announce lunch. "I'll save you a seat." Suzanne laughed, joining the crowd heading toward the dining hall.
> I caught up to Mary.
> "You've got to help me, Frank. I can't have Richard running around the festival. He could hurt somebody, destroy an instrument."
> "I've seen Richard. He could destroy an entire building."
> "He must have broken through his pen. Or somebody let him out."
> We cut a short corner around the showers and turned left at the old tractor shed. Ten yards beyond the tractor shed stood the pigpen. The only way you could miss it was if you'd lost all sense of smell. In the Midwest smart farmers located pigpens east of the house. Downwind. Mary's farm had once belonged to a smart farmer.

A cupola topped the roof of the low shelter inside the pigpen. The way I figured it, some nineteenth-century farmer had come west to Iroquois County, erected the most serious building first — the barn — then abandoned the county to head west again. Somebody else had come by and started erecting outbuildings, each with a cupola.

The pigpen door was still fastened. I had seen no pig inside the pen on my earlier trips: it must have been in its shed when I walked by. Probably admiring the cupola from the inside.

"Here's the problem," I called. A bottom board had rotted away. A closer look told me it was chewed through, not rotted. Richard was one hungry porker.

Mary hurried around to examine the board. "You've got to fix it."

I looked at her to see if she was serious.

She was.

"You're the carpenter!" she said, reading my expression.

"Think again."

"Well, but, Frank — you've *got* to fix it. Who else can I count on? What if Richard harms someone? I mean, he *is* big."

"I'll fix it right after lunch," I grumbled.

"Maybe you should fix it now," she suggested. "I don't know where Richard is or what he's doing."

"Creek," I replied, walking away from the pigpen. "Wallowing."

A dark thought ran around my brain: what if she hired me mainly to get a carpenter, cheap? I turned to look at her. "You don't know much about pigs, do you?"

"Richard's an indoor pig. I wasn't sure about putting him outside, but I couldn't very well keep him in the house during the festival, could I?"

"An indoor pig," I repeated.

"Yes, a pet. Pigs are very intelligent animals. They—"

"I know all that," I interrupted. "I'm surprised he hasn't crashed through the floor boards."

"I keep him in the back room, a new addition. It's concrete. Are you going to fix the pen after lunch?" She huffed to keep up with me.

I gritted my teeth. "Yes."

Between the pig's first spontaneous appearance in chapter three and its second mention in that same chapter, the same subconscious which created the pig also revealed to me the pig's name and personality: Richard sought escape and adventure. But what I learned about Richard is little compared to what Frank Dragovic learned. He learned that Mary Ployd would take advantage of his carpenter "disguise" and have him do carpentry work around the farm, at no pay — during the time Frank thinks he needs to be walking the grounds and observing the suspects. This conflict between Frank and Mary crops up several times in the book. As does Richard.

My subconscious, it turns out, served me well, because when people read *Sound Proof*, they almost always tell me, "I loved the pig!" So, while most of the work you do on creating characters will require weeks or months of thinking, note-taking, analyzing, and researching, some of the work will be more intuitive — it will come to you instinctively, possibly when you aren't expecting it.

Take advantage of that: trust your subconscious.

5

Minor Characters

Novels contain minor characters as well as major ones, and while it's not necessary for a writer to know as much about the minor characters as about the major ones, it's still necessary to know something about them. Mainly, it's necessary to know their function in the plot.

To Name or Not to Name

There are two levels of minor characters. The first kind play a role in the book. They speak, they act, they interact with the protagonist. Because they speak, act, and interact, a writer will think about these minor characters and develop them to a certain degree.

The second kind of minor characters are those who have one short function in the novel and aren't heard from again. Or if they're heard from again, it's merely in the same capacity or function as they first appeared. You might consider these to be minor-minor characters. In *Dirty Proof* the doorman of the building Suzanne lives in falls into that category, as do several of Suzanne's fellow typesetters. In *Sound Proof* I usually have Frank refer to the sheriff's deputy as "the deputy" rather than by name. The job description is easy for readers to remember, especially in a novel that contains many characters.

Whether or not to name minor characters is a difficulty all writers face. Obviously the minor characters who speak, act, and interact with the hero need names. But what about the minor-minor ones, such as the doorman or deputy?

The rule-of-thumb I try to follow in writing a mystery is: what would my protagonist observe and need to know? How would he behave? If my hero were a cop investigating a case, I think he would take down the name of practically every character he encountered. Although, in order to not burden the reader with unnecessary details, this could be written as "I wrote her name in my notebook." If the point of view is third person: "Khrank wrote the doorman's name in his notebook, right under the name of the concierge." But if, later, this doorman were to play a role in the book, perhaps because his last name turned out to be the same as the last name of the murder victim's brother-in-law, then the writer needs to give the name as the protagonist writes it down — else the writer wouldn't be playing fair with the reader.

If your hero is an amateur detective, whether or not she notes or writes down or remembers the name of the doorman or the concierge all depends on how observant she is, how conscious she is of gathering evidence, whether or not she intends to question this person, and a whole host of other things. An amateur detective doesn't have the status, authority, or training of a member of the police force, nor that of a private investigator (who has had training). In some ways you have more freedom to allow your protagonist to slip up when you're writing about an amateur detective. Or to be way nosier than even a private detective might be.

How you write about your minor characters depends on who is telling the story (point of view will be discussed in a later chapter) and what kind of detective she is. If you stay true to what your hero would say and do and observe, you will name or not name your minor characters appropriately.

Function of Each Character

Minor characters serve a function in the novel. They might be used to move the plot forward by providing information, for example, or by taking actions that clarify things. Or by saying something relevant, perhaps without knowing that they've done so.

They can also be used to complicate the plot, throwing a monkey wrench into things, perhaps sending the chase off in a different direction. Further, they can be used to shed light on other characters, either by being similar or by being very different. Minor characters can also be used to elucidate and enhance the setting.

As you create minor characters, you will find yourself giving some of them names and even occupations. Perhaps you know the physical description of some of them, but not all of them. Let your instincts guide you in this respect, as they guided me. Here are a few of the minor characters in *Sound Proof,* with notes I made before I began writing the novel.

Personnel
Nola Grayson — Mary's attorney, conference go-to person
Function: reflects light on Shelby Stubbs; reveals what could be a motive for murder; is a contrast to Mary

Teachers
Kofi Quay — African drummer
Function: as an outsider to American culture, he comments on that culture; he quietly teaches others, including Frank, the power of music

Students
Cindy Ruffo — mountain dulcimer player
Function: adds to the setting by her background and behavior

Vendors
Kim Oberfeld — sells fiddles, autoharps, guitars
Function: adds to the setting; adds to plot advancement by giving Frank information

Because these minor characters speak, act, and interact with Frank Dragovic during the course of *Sound Proof,* I had to flesh them out. I needed to know some of their externals and internals: personality and character. Here are my notes on Cindy Ruffo:

Students
Cindy Ruffo — mountain dulcimer player — has a family, husband and seven children, from Missouri, drives an old van she lives out of during the festival, makes her own clothes, religious, believes in the devil, she saves her money (of which there is very little) in order to come to Midwest Music Madness once a year. She saved her money to buy a beautiful mountain dulcimer by a well-

known luthier: this instrument was stolen the second year of Midwest Music Madness.

As my notes indicate, I created minor character Cindy Ruffo for several different reasons. I wanted to show that many people who play folk music and attend festivals are poor people: music is a joy they can create for themselves and in company with others. This aspect of Cindy contributes to the setting of *Sound Proof*. I also wanted to show how important a musician's instrument is to him or her, whether that person is rich or poor. The instrument has a personality and a life for the musician, and the loss of an instrument (especially through theft) is a physical and emotional blow. The instrument is mourned. Sometimes avenged. In the face of murder (that of Shelby Stubbs), some readers may cast aside any concerns about theft. But I wanted Frank's initial job — finding the instrument thief — to remain important. The more the reader feels empathy for Cindy, the less the reader will undervalue Frank's search for the thief. Finally, at many of the musical festivals I attended there was always a small group which played and sang religious songs, sometimes all night long. Cindy helps me show that segment of the folk music tribe. In short, Cindy is not only a developed minor character in *Sound Proof*, she serves certain story and setting purposes.

When creating minor characters, ask yourself what purpose each one serves. To complicate the plot? To shine light on a problem? To enrich the setting? In a mystery it's very easy to create minor characters who serve only the purpose of providing information that the detective needs. Try to make your minor characters serve more functions than that single one.

Combining Characters

In creating minor characters (and major ones, too), you might, in the planning stages of your novel, end up creating too many. Not too many for the pages of the novel to handle: novels come in all sizes. But too many for readers to handle. When you give your novel over for critique, listen to whether people are confused by certain characters. Usually the reader will say something like, "I couldn't keep A and B straight." Or, "I couldn't tell U and V apart." Or, "I kept forgetting who Z was."

Such remarks could indicate that you need to strengthen the characterization of the characters in question: make these novel people come to life. Or such remarks could mean that you have too many characters serving identical functions.

After I finished *Sound Proof* I asked readers to critique it. And one of the most frequent remarks I received was that readers found it difficult to distinguish between various minor characters. (Remember: I needed more minor characters than you will probably ever need, because I was writing about a festival.)

Now, it's a fact of life that the characters you as a writer create are real, vivid, and utterly distinct to you. But not necessarily to the reader. I know this because when I'm a reader, I often find myself confused by characters I can't remember or distinguish. So as a writer, I remembered my experiences as a reader, and when I rewrote *Sound Proof* I conflated two major characters into one. I also conflated two minor characters into one. And I totally deleted four other minor characters. Here are my rewrite notes:

Guy and Max — combine into one character
Jing and Bliss — combine into one character
Paul — delete
Destry — delete
Abby — delete
Penna — delete

Six months after I rewrote *Sound Proof*, I had *no idea* who the deleted characters had been or what function they had served. Zero idea. In retrospect, I didn't need these characters at all. You too, either in your initial writing (moving the story from notecard or outline stage to manuscript stage) or in your rewriting, may find the need to combine either major or minor characters. If some instinct tells you to do so, I highly advise doing it. Better to have five minor characters, each of whom the reader finds memorable, than to have fifteen whom the reader fails to recognize.

6

Character Tags

In the previous chapter I mentioned that while your characters are very vivid and distinct to you, they aren't always so to your reader. In fact, readers need a lot of help keeping your characters straight — just as you might need a lot of help if you entered a room of twenty people you had never met before, and each introduced himself as you walked around the room once. By the time you returned to the first person you had met, how many of those twenty people would you remember by name, by profession, and by purpose (why they were there)? Chances are high you wouldn't remember all twenty.

So imagine the dilemma readers face when a character who appears in chapters one and two disappears from the book for a while, only to return in chapter thirteen. If the writer mentions this character by name only, the reader often won't remember who this person is.

At that point some readers will stop reading and begin flipping backward through the pages, trying to find a previous reference to this character in order to remember who she is. Others may look for a "cast of characters" listing in the front of the book. Just about every reader who can't remember a character will not blame herself: she will blame you, the writer. The complaint of "I can't keep the characters straight" is *not* a self-admonition: it's a complaint against the writer. Readers (and rightly so) want you, the writer, to help them remember who the various major and minor characters are.

Character Tags as Identification

Luckily, writers have invented ways of doing this, and these ways are called *tags*. You've encountered tags in museums, garage sales, and maybe even flea markets: *This hand-cranked box was used for grinding whole coffee beans. Sometimes it was used to grind small amounts of corn.*

A tag, then, is a label or description attached to something for the purpose of identification. In real life tags might be small stiff-paper rectangles, sometimes with strings attached. In fiction, tags are words or phrases "attached" to a character each time or most of the times the character appears.

Tags don't start out being tags. They start out simply as part of your description of a person: his or her physical appearance, dress, quality of voice, mannerisms, gestures, eyes, hair, and so on. But when you begin to repeat one or more of these initial descriptions, you are using them as tags: labels that help readers remember who this person is.

When Frank Dragovic first meets Lafayette Wafer (one of the suspects for instrument theft), Lafayette is holding a bowed psaltry. (Later in the book Frank describes the bowed psaltry in detail.) Shelby Stubbs, who will be murdered by the end of the day, makes a point of insulting both Lafayette and the bowed psaltry.

> Lafayette Wafer bounced up and down in indignation. He was another one to watch. "I paid to play the bowed psaltry in Waydell's class, and now Shelby—"
>
> "The *bowed psaltry!*" roared Stubbs. "I liked it better when you scratched away on that miserable little fiddle of yours, Lafayette. The bowed psaltry ain't even a real instrument! It's a Christmas tree gone bad! *No* instrument — I repeat, *no* instrument — deserves to be in a class with a bowed psaltry." He shuddered dramatically. "Compared to that thing, the hurdy-gurdy sounds good."

From the moment he's introduced (page four), Lafayette is identified partly by the instrument he plays. Other musicians in the book are also identified by the instruments they play and carry around. Guy Dufour, for example, carries around a heavy (thirty-some pounds) hammered dulcimer. After that initial encounter, Lafayette appears again seven pages later:

> Lafayette Wafer, another suspect, shuffled across the floor with bowed psaltry in hand. "You should know better than to leave your autoharp alone overnight," he told her as he examined a Leatherman tool that hung from his belt. Guy wore a similar small tool on his belt. I guess stringed instruments needed frequent repair.

Of course there's more to any character than a single item he or she carries around. Some of Lafayette's other distinguishing features are his reedy voice, his wispy beard, his body odor, and his scruffy clothing. Early on Frank notes these en masse, but later in the book he mentions one or two as character tags:

> "Nobody does," Lafayette muttered into his iced tea. His skin was pale, his sharply pointed nose covered with burst capillaries. I caught the whiff of alcohol when I leaned his way. Also the odor of stale sweat. His clothes, old khakis cut off below the knee, a graying T-shirt, and old leather sandals, spoke of neglect. Pushing his tea away, Lafayette fidgeted with the multiple parts of his Leatherman — screwdriver, awl, wire cutter, pliers, saw, scissors.

Later in the book, as Frank is walking the grounds of Mary Ployd's farm, he hears a sound he can't immediately identify:

> Skittering above the drumming came a high, thin screech. Mosquitoes? My eyes turned toward the creek. Under the shade of the massive black walnut tree sat Lafayette Wafer, bowing his psaltry.
> Lafayette was on Mary's list of five prime suspects. I walked over to him.
> He lifted his head at my approach. Wrinkled his pointed nose, tensed his bony shoulders. His pale skin was lightly freckled, his goatee brown and wispy.

Each of the passages I've quoted is from the beginning of *Sound Proof*, within the first thirty-five pages. Although I used character tags throughout the novel, I used more of them in the first half of the book, where the reader's need to distinguish one character from another is greatest. The tag reminders help readers remember and distinguish.

Not all of the characters in *Sound Proof* carry instruments with them. Nola Grayson, Mary's attorney and festival organizer, does not. For her I created other tags:

> Unlike most of the people present, she wasn't dressed casually. In addition to a gray linen suit she wore T-strap shoes, gold earrings, bracelets, and rings. Her toenails and fingernails were blood red. Seriously

overweight, she moved slowly. I figured she'd be pretty conspicuous walking around with somebody else's instrument: people would have remembered seeing her. Still, Nola was intelligent and efficient, and I didn't rule her out altogether.

Her weight, her jewelry, and her business suits are tags for Nola Grayson, helping set her apart from the rest of the characters, none of whom wear business suits. But Nola's speech patterns also act as character tags. She is educated and she practices law: her speech pattern is different from those of the other characters.

"Good morning, Frank. If the sheriff has been questioning you and you'd like me present the next time he does, I'll be happy to sit in. You have the right to have an attorney present when questioned by the police." Nola was, as always, professional.

When you're thinking of how to describe one of your characters, think also of what you'll be able to use as tags. Is it someone's wild red hair? Habitual cough? Overused verbal crutch such as *dude, like,* or *no problem?* Unconscious habits, such as the gesture of rubbing one's palms together, or constantly pushing up the sleeves of one's shirt or sweater?

Whatever it is you decide upon as a character tag, keep in mind that you will be able to use these tags for two purposes, not just one.

Character Tags for Character

In addition to helping readers remember who a character is, tags also work to show readers what a character is like. In other words, tags help characterize your fictional people. Perhaps you have a character who is cocksure of himself: presumptuously or arrogantly confident. Maybe he has connections with criminals. You might have him, whenever he meets somebody, form his hand into the shape of a gun, aim it at the person he encounters, and "pull" the trigger. This is not only rude, it's aggressive and possibly threatening. And if after he pulls the trigger, he aims the gun upward and blows the smoke away (all using hand gestures, not an actual weapon), the reader can see how arrogant and insensitive the character is.

If you want to show that a character is always asserting her will over others, you would give her appropriate character tags. In bringing out this aspect of Mary Ployd's character, I described her gait as a march or forceful stride, and I gave her the gesture of placing her hands in front of her, palms down, then quickly sweeping them to the side, to indicate *Conversation over and done with. I won't hear any more on this subject!*

Shelby Stubbs also asserts his will over others, from page one until his death. Two tags I gave him are that he is always hitching up his pants (a kind of arrogant gesture, a reminder to others that he is a male animal and might respond aggressively), and that he always says "No sir" to any argument. The "No sir" is not a phrase of respect, but a phrase cutting off any further discussion: *No, that's final. Over and done with. Get out of here!*

>Shelby Stubbs stepped onto a bale of straw and looked down on the group of musicians. I leaned against a porch rail and watched everything in sight. Even Stubbs, though he wasn't the thief.
>
>Stubbs hooked a thumb through his belt, puffed out his chest, and repeated his announcement. "No sir. Absolutely not." This was directed at Vance Jurasek, who was balancing a string bass on its endpin. "Only fiddles, guitars, and banjos," Stubbs lectured. "No other instruments allowed. That's 'cause no other instruments belong."
>
>"You're kidding." Jurasek settled his bass against the rail and scowled.
>
>"No sir. You don't see a bass in old-time music. It's not traditional. You never saw an old-time player carrying a bass around. No bass in my class."
>
>Jurasek, his thin ponytail hanging limp in the prairie heat, waved a small emerald-green instrument bag at Stubbs. "You'll accept a mandolin, though, right? Bill Monroe played the mandolin."
>
>Stubbs glared. "Don't tell me what Bill Monroe played. I don't dispute that mandolins have a *fine* sound. Fine for bluegrass. But they don't belong in old-time music. 'Sides, I heard you playing that mandolin as we

drove in, and either you or the instrument is off key."
Face flushed, Jurasek shot Stubbs a murderous look.

Tags and Tension

Tags, as I've indicated, help readers distinguish one character from another. And they help tell readers something about the character. In addition, tags can sometimes be used to create tension in a novel, by annoying or irritating another character. Imagine how irritated you could become if every time you saw Mickey he pointed a symbolic imaginary gun (his fingers) at you, pulled the trigger, and blew the smoke away. Maybe it wouldn't bother you most of the time, but there would be occasions when you were tired, upset, or angry about something else, and that gesture just might be the last straw. Especially in tense situations, gestures, coughs, speech habits — these little things can annoy others.

And speaking of annoying others, keep in mind that while you want to use tags to help the reader identify your characters, don't get carried away. Using a tag too often can annoy your reader to no end. At some point the reader *knows* who your characters are and probably wants to read *without* reading the tag. Too much of a good thing can turn into a bad thing.

My advice is :

> (1) create good tags — tags that are visual for the reader, immediately identifiable
> (2) create tags that help characterize your fictional person
> (3) use these tags often in the first third of the novel then taper off after that
> (4) reintroduce the tag with the character any time that character hasn't been on the scene for the last couple of chapters, or perhaps the last 30 or 40 pages

Speech Tags

There is one other kind of "tag" that exists in fiction and

nonfiction, and that's the speech tag — words such as *she said* and *he said* that tell readers which character is speaking.

Some writers think they can write more vividly if they use a thesaurus's worth of synonyms for *said*. Words such as *uttered, spoke, pronounced, commented, responded, grumbled, vocalized, mentioned, remarked*. But the fact is, the words *he said* and *she said* used repeatedly bother the writer far more than they bother the reader: if they bother the reader at all. The word *said* is so innocuous that readers blitz by it to get to the next line.

Readers will, however, notice if you use too many synonyms for *said*, too often. Your text will read as unnatural. What's "natural" to a reader of fiction is *said*, not a host of synonyms that call attention to themselves. Which is not to say that you should *never* use synonyms for *said*. Use them, but use them judiciously, maybe one every third or fourth page. Such intermittent use will provide a pleasant sparkle for the reader (whereas a host of synonyms one after the other will bombard the reader).

And while I'm on the subject of speech tags, let me say that my preference as a reader is that lines of dialogue without speech attribution do not go on, back and forth, for more than three lines — four, tops. In theory it's easy to say that if there are two speakers, it's obvious which line of dialogue belongs to which speaker. But in practice, this isn't so easy. If you're in doubt about whether your dialogue has gone on too long without an attribution, ask several people to read the passage and mark where they lose track of who the speaker is. Also, whenever you're reading a novel in which you lose track of who the speaker is, take note of why you lost track — and avoid that particular situation in your own writing.

Setting, Including Scene of the Crime

Some writers are great at creating setting, others are indifferent to it. Some are great at all three aspects of setting, some at one or perhaps two. This reflects how different we all are. Some of us are very conscious about clothing styles, others aren't. Some of us are always *au courant* with the latest slang or buzz words, others aren't. Some observe architecture, or trees, or house interiors in detail. Others don't.

But no matter what we're like in real life, in the world of fiction it's necessary for a writer to be aware of setting — of creating it and maintaining it. Of making it come alive for the reader. For the fact is, one of the great vicarious pleasures readers get from fiction is the pleasure of setting: people enjoy learning about other places, other times, and other cultures through fiction.

Setting: Place, Time, Culture

Setting consists of the place or spot where a story takes place; the time when it takes place; and the culture in which it takes place. A mystery could take place in the Adirondack Mountains of New York. That's the spot on Earth where the story is set. (Stories need not be set on Earth, of course.) The story could take place now, in the 21st century. Or it could take place in the 19th century, during the days of the Underground Railroad. Or earlier, during the days of the French and Indian War. Or even earlier, when Indian tribes lived free of Europeans.

The cultural setting could be any of the above-mentioned. It could be Dutch-Americans whose families have lived in the region for over 200 years. It could be about criminals who run meth labs. It could be about amusement park owners.

In mystery novels as in other novels, these three aspects of setting can be equally developed, or one or two can be developed more than the others. But I can't imagine a novel in which they wouldn't all be present.

Dirty Proof takes place in the 1970s, in Chicago, in the culture of the newspaper publishing industry: mainly in the composing room, where typesetters worked.

Sound Proof, as you know by now, takes place in the current era (say early 21st century) in Iroquois County, Illinois, on a farm during an old-time music festival called Midwest Music Madness. The culture it takes place in is the culture of folk music or, more specifically, what's called old-time music (the kind of music played by the Carter Family and by Doc Watson and John Hartford, for example).

As I explained in an earlier chapter, setting is very important to me, and it comes to me at the same time as do plot and character. In the very first page of *Sound Proof*, the culture aspect of the setting is prominent:

> Shelby Stubbs stepped onto a bale of straw and looked down on the group of musicians. I leaned against a porch rail and watched everything in sight. Even Stubbs, though he wasn't the thief.
> Stubbs hooked a thumb through his belt, puffed out his chest, and repeated his announcement. "No sir. Absolutely not." This was directed at Vance Jurasek, who was balancing a string bass on its endpin. "Only fiddles, guitars, and banjos," Stubbs lectured. "No other instruments allowed. That's 'cause no other instruments belong."
> "You're kidding." Jurasek settled his bass against the rail and scowled.
> "No sir. You don't see a bass in old-time music. It's not traditional. You never saw an old-time player carrying a bass around. No bass in my class."

Researching Setting

In developing setting you might end up doing research in several different ways: travel, internet, library, or others. If your mystery is set in the past you're probably aware that today there are wonderful web sites through which a visitor can see photos of buildings, rooms, clothing, and many other artifacts of previous eras. Research your setting well before you actually sit down to write — that way, details about the setting will be in your mind and will emerge in your writing. It's easier to feel yourself inside the setting from the start, rather than to have to "add" setting during the rewrite. The first is organic, the second artificial.

Speaking of setting and research, let me say that a wise and conscientious writer researches any aspect of his novel that he isn't 100% certain about. Take, for example, the murder weapon. If it's a gun, you had better be certain what kind of gun it is and how it works. Readers will know instantly if you've said something wrong about the gun. The same is true for poisons or any murder method: research it first . . . in books, articles, or online. If you can, interview experts on the subject.

Back to setting. I've already told you that *Sound Proof* sprang out of the fact that I accompanied my husband to many old-time music festivals and observed and absorbed what I saw and heard. As for the farm aspect of the setting, I spent most of my childhood on a dairy farm in Ohio. But Ohio is not Illinois, and so before I began to write *Sound Proof* I traveled to Iroquois County, Illinois. I drove up and down the rural roads. I drove through the towns. I ate lunch in one of them. I jotted down notes on the town buildings, the railroads, the bus depots, the barns, the silos, the fields, the farmhouses, the drainage ditches. I took photos. I typed notes and printed them out and had them alongside me as I wrote, so that I could incorporate them throughout the book.

There is, however, a great danger in having copious notes on any single aspect of your story. The danger is that because you did the work garnering this information, and because you are excited about it, you will cram it into your novel.

Don't.

Readers like details. They like a setting to come alive for them. But what they really, really *love* is dialogue and action. Setting is neither dialogue nor action. So use what you know about your setting sensibly.

Below is a single page from my four single-spaced pages of Iroquois County research notes. The observations in boldfaced type are the ones I used as part of the setting — the others I didn't use at all. I hope this drives home the point that research results work best when used selectively.

cupolas on barns, even on sheds and on police station
third-floor of a farmhouse has stained glass windows
saloon with Bud Light sign overhead and Old Style sign on side
saloon made of red brick
hip roof with cupola
saloon serves burgers and beer
post office is on Main Street
saloon is on Main Street
pickup trucks, most of them American makes
black-eyed susans everywhere
many, many pole barns in addition to the main barns
abandoned buildings
grain storage silos
L-shaped porches on many farmhouses
Depot Street, Church Street, Main Street
1st, 2nd, 3rd, 4th streets
circle of rocks in ditch, probably thrown out of the field by a farmer
lots of one-and-a-half-lane dirt roads, especially running alongside cornfields

Sketching Setting

One other thing I did in developing the setting for *Sound*

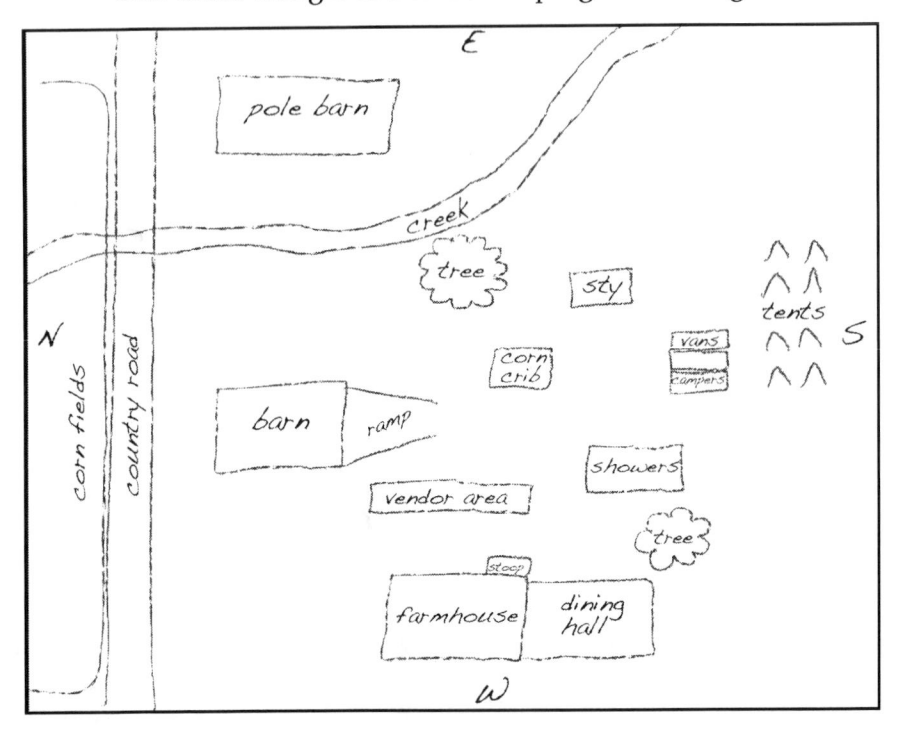

Proof was to draw a sketch showing me where the buildings were in relationship to one another.

I kept this sketch alongside my desk while I wrote perhaps the first third of the book. Soon I knew Mary's farm and the festival grounds so well that I didn't need the sketch: the mental image was imprinted on my brain.

In writing *Dirty Proof* I had no such sketch. That's because *Dirty Proof* took place in a wide variety of places within Chicago, and Chicago is a real place. Mary Ployd's farm, however, is not real. With an invented setting, the temptation is to write the story and occasionally throw in something about the surroundings. But I felt that method wouldn't bring the setting to life. Because the story is told in the first-person point of view, I wanted to imagine what Frank Dragovic would see as he walked the grounds.

Here are three examples of how setting appears in *Sound Proof*.

> Mary's barn brought back these memories. Entering her barn through the south side, I noticed that all six double doors — south, east, and north — were rolled back, the few windows propped open with sticks. The entire bottom floor hosted the old-time ensemble class. Clustered around a pine stage built against the north wall, most of the students perched on rusty folding chairs. Others took a big chance with chairs cobbled together out of branches and twigs. I suspected Mary might host a rustic furniture festival during the winter.

. . .

> Like the outbuildings, the barn was aligned with its long sides facing east and west. Along its old stone perimeter I looked for possible hiding places, checking for chinks below, loose boards above. If I were the thief, I'd swipe an instrument and hide it immediately, so I couldn't be caught with it.
>
> Mary's barn was in serious need of painting. Its weathered gray wood was probably last painted when Bob Dylan was a teen. Back in Chicago the aged siding would fetch a fortune as ambience in a restaurant or private home. The barn's east wall faced a small creek, Raccoon Run. No hiding places I could see. And the south wall was unlikely because it could be seen from the dining

hall. High above me, below the peak of the gambrel roof, the hayloft door stood open. Music from a guitar class drifted down.

. . .

No time for a shower. I wondered which was more socially unacceptable: showing up late the first day of class, or smelling like a pig sty. Wafting eau de swine in all directions, I hurried toward the pole barn.

Farmers like my Uncle Rudy and whoever had owned Mary's land before her constructed pole barns quickly and cheaply: one story high, gable roof, round poles as the main structural support, siding hung from two-by-fours. The life expectancy of such barns was thirty or forty years: a one-generation solution to hay and machine storage problems. Mary's pole barn, its two short sides sagging toward each other, stood at the brink of its life cycle. One long side slumped on its own door, and a lone, dust-covered window blended in with the weathered wood.

Between the pigpen and the pole barn, clumps of butterfly milkweed still bloomed in the blazing sun. I wondered if Mary had considered restoring these few acres to prairie: it could be an additional attraction of her festival.

In each of these paragraphs I as the writer knew where Frank was within the setting and what he saw. Having the sketch helped me.

By the time I got to the storm scene in chapter eighteen (a critical situation that reveals much about the various characters and leads to a partial solution to one of the mysteries), I knew my setting so well that I could feel Frank moving through it.

"Attention, attention!" she continued. "Fonnie Sheffler is missing from the old-time ensemble group."

There was a general shuffling, people looking left and right and all around, as if the missing person had simply failed to report to the right group. During these few seconds of confusion Fonnie herself staggered in through the southern doors. "Where were you?" demanded Vance. "We were worried about you."

"Sorry," she gasped. "I wanted to secure my camper." She struggled for more breath. "It's really bad out there."

"Fonnie has been found!" shouted Mary. "Lafayette Wafer is also missing from the old-time ensemble group. Has anybody seen Lafayette?"

We looked around again, and then we looked toward the south door, as if Lafayette would repeat Fonnie's trick of appearing out of the blue. In this case the black.

Once it was clear that Lafayette wasn't there, Mary asked if anybody knew where he was. Voices offered facts, opinions, judgments.

"I saw him around four o'clock," Cindy called out. "He said a tune was calling him."

"That's right," shouted Vance. "He was heading toward the big tree by the creek."

"But it was already starting to rain," Cindy yelled. "He might have gone to the pole barn."

Mary repeated these remarks to all over the microphone and asked if any of us had seen Lafayette after that time. Hearing her was becoming more and more difficult in the thunder. I walked over to Suzanne and took the flashlight and first-aid kit from her backpack. She had packed our rain jackets and I pulled mine on.

"Where are you going?" she asked, a note of panic in her voice.

"The pole barn."

"No!" She grabbed my arm. "Frank, don't go."

I shook my head. "I've got to."

"For who?" demanded Booker, watching me. "Lafayette?"

I stuffed the first-aid kit in a pocket and gripped the flashlight.

"Don't do it, man." Booker placed a hand on my shoulder. "It's too dangerous."

I moved to leave but Booker pushed me back. "No! Let the little rat drown! He doesn't deserve saving."

Knowing the physical setting well helped me write this scene. And knowing the setting also helped Frank find his way back from the pole barn. Setting is not just something a writer puts into a book: it's something the book's characters live in. That's why it's important for you to make the setting visible to the reader. And I mean cultural setting as well as physical setting.

Connections with Setting

Setting is connected to the story experience in three different ways. First there's the connection between the writer and the setting. The writer works to make the setting come alive, especially since readers love learning vicariously.

Second, there's the connection between the reader and the setting. Readers want to experience the setting of a book, particularly if it's a world they know little about (as is, for example, the world of old-time music). But readers in general don't want long descriptions of setting, so writers work to bring the setting to life in ways other than long descriptions. I'll discuss how this is done in the chapter on description.

Third, there's the connection between the characters and the setting, particularly between the protagonist and the setting. Is the setting in the protagonist's wheelhouse, so to speak? Does he know it well, function in it well? Or is he a fish out of water, totally lost in this setting? The connection between the hero and the setting is important for you to consider, because it will determine the hero's attitude and actions and observations and maybe even success or failure.

In writing *Sound Proof* I wanted Frank Dragovic to be unfamiliar with old-time music (though Suzanne is familiar with it). In a way, I was giving him a handicap in solving the murder of an old-time musician, probably *by* an old-time musician. Frank is an outsider with no knowledge of musical terms or traditions or fingerings of stringed instruments. It's good to give your characters weaknesses, sometimes several kinds of weaknesses. Admittedly, not knowing old-time music isn't considered much of a weakness by most people, but it does put Frank at a disadvantage, and that makes him more human. It also means that some of the characters who do know old-time music will underestimate Frank's abilities: humans have a tendency to think that those inside a particular group are better or smarter than those outside it.

At the same time, I didn't want to make Frank an outsider to everything except detection, so I made him familiar with farms and barns and farm animals. Even though he's a city person, born and raised in Chicago, I had him spend his summers on his uncle's farm in Galesburg, Illinois. Because of this Frank moves through the setting confidently and comfortably, and this means he can spend his psychic energy observing what he as a detective needs to observe.

I notice that in my first novel I also made Frank an outsider to typesetting and the composing room. It could be that I like to treat the reader to unusual settings and place my hero in unusual settings — just so that, despite the setting, he can triumph.

Scene of the Crime

In some mysteries the scene of the crime is more important than in others. Police procedurals, for example, often give minute details about the scene of the crime because it's the job of the crime scene specialists to gather evidence that will help detectives interpret the way the crime was committed and what kind of person did it. If you read police procedurals, you'll be familiar with how scene-of-the-crime is developed. Many thrillers also show and develop scene-of-the-crime details.

Whether those who write private eye or amateur detective fiction need to develop the scene of the crime depends on the answer to a question I raised earlier in this book: does the crime occur during the course of the novel, or has it already occurred when the book opens? In *Dirty Proof* the murder of Ralph Blasingame has already occurred before the first page of the novel. But any self-respecting detective would want to investigate the scene of the crime, even if the crime had occurred months or years ago. One of the first things Frank does in *Dirty Proof* is walk through the scene of the crime. In doing so he reaches certain conclusions about the murder.

In *Sound Proof* the murder occurs at the end of the first day of the five-day music festival, so in this book I needed to show the scene of the crime. In order to do so I had to know what the physical place of the crime looked like. I had to know (of course!) who the killer was and how he committed the crime. I had to know (and this is visually important) what people who entered the scene of the crime would see. And: I had to plant important clues and/or important misdirections — pieces of the scene that might lead the protagonist and/or the police in the wrong direction.

Here's how the reader experiences the scene of the crime in *Sound Proof,* through the eyes of Frank Dragovic.

The moaning came from Bliss.

Shelby Stubbs lay on the couch of his RV, his head smashed in, blood splattered on both couch and wall. I checked his pulse just to make sure. Dead. The body was still warm, but on a night like this that meant little.

Only two places to sit: up front in the driver and passenger compartments, or in the dinette directly across from Stubbs' body. I moved Bliss toward the front of the vehicle, pulled aside the pleated curtains separating the front from the back, and sat her in the passenger seat. "Stay here," I said, hooking back the curtains so I could keep an eye on her.

A cell phone rested on the sink counter. I took a kerchief out of my shorts, held the phone with it and dialed 911. Behind me, the microwave clock read 3:30 A.M. Turning away from Bliss I reported the murder, then replaced the phone on the counter. I thought of calling Mary but decided against it for the time being.

"Somebody will be here soon," I told Bliss. She was shaking. "Can you hold on?"

She stared out the window into the dark. When I arrived, she had been moaning in the doorway.

I returned to the living quarters, if they could still be called that, and looked around. One of the dinette benches held Bliss's mountain dulcimer case, a couple of small cosmetic bags, and an African drum. One of Kofi's drums, I was sure. On the other bench lay a bright red fiddle.

The fiddle was in fine fettle — except for its four strings, which somebody had snipped off and twisted round and round the fiddle's neck, as if strangling it. I looked but didn't touch. A bow lay on the floor. I squatted to examine it, expecting to find its horsehairs cut through, but the bow looked fine.

The red fiddle wasn't the one Stubbs' had played in class. That had been the $20,000 fiddle and the $10,000 bow Mary wanted safe at all costs. I looked around for his black fiddle case. Using the kerchief, I lifted the handles of storage areas, peeking inside. No fiddle case. No $20,000 fiddle. No $10,000 bow. In fact, there was no fiddle case anywhere, not even for the strangled red fiddle.

I rubbed my forehead with both hands. Stolen hurdy-gurdy, stolen fiddle and bow, and a murdered man. I was standing at the plate looking as the strikes blew by me.

And something else was missing.

The murder weapon.

Stubbs' head was smashed in, his skull cracked wide open. Flecks of brain dotted the couch and the window above it. As far as I could see, no weapon in sight.

I went to sit in the driver seat. "Tell me what happened," I said.

"Is he dead?" Bliss breathed.

"Yes. Where were you?"

She stared at me without answering.

Complications at the Scene of the Crime

As you can tell from reading this scene, I'm not a techno-type writer (or reader). That is, I don't concentrate on small technical details or expert technical knowledge for the murders in my mysteries. The murders are somewhat basic. But that doesn't mean I can't introduce complications into the scene of the crime.

The scene above contains the following evidence and complications:

(1) Stubbs was murdered with a blunt instrument.
(2) But that instrument is not present at the scene of the crime when Frank arrives.
(3) One of Stubbs' prized fiddles, a red one, has had its strings cut, and the strings have been wound and twisted around the neck of the fiddle.
(4) Stubbs' main fiddle and bow, both very expensive, both insured, are missing.
(5) No fiddle cases are present on the scene of the crime.

My purpose in creating these details at the scene of the crime was to complicate matters, specifically to suggest that the person who murdered Stubbs may have been the same person who was stealing stringed instruments — else why would Stubbs' expensive fiddle and bow be missing?

I used a blunt instrument as the murder weapon in order to throw suspicion on those characters who had been using hammers earlier that day. These include Mary Ployd, Raven Hook, Jeff Glover, Kim Oberfeld, and Frank Dragovic (though I hope the reader does not suspect Frank!)

I used the cut fiddle strings to throw suspicion on those characters who had been using Leatherman tools on Monday. These include Lafayette Wafer and Guy Dufour.

I used the fact that one fiddle was stolen while the other wasn't stolen (but was mutilated) to throw confusion over what happened and why.

I'lll have more to say about the planting of clues and the casting of suspicion in later chapters.

Point of View

Along with plot, characters, and setting, point of view is one of the four fundamental choices a writer makes in creating her story. Many writers, both beginning and experienced, consider point of view the most difficult decision to make in telling the story.

Point of view is the outlook from which the story is told. Or, to put it another way, it's the character or characters within the story from whose eyes we "see" the story.

Writers and teachers who talk about point of view may differ on how many points of view there are to choose from, or what the subdivisions are. So what I have to say may vary slightly from what other authors have to say. For my purposes, I classify point of view (commonly abbreviated as POV) into three main choices.

> **First Person**
> > **First Person Singular**
> > **First Person Multiple**
> > **First Person Plural**
>
> **Second Person**
>
> **Third Person**
> > **Third Person Limited**
> > **Third Person Multiple**
> > **Third Person Omniscient**

Some writers (more than you would think) have difficulty comprehending point of view. They choose one and proceed with it, but then within the story they violate that point of view. This violation jolts discerning readers out of the story immediately. It's as if readers have been journeying a smooth highway in a limousine, enjoying the beautiful view, chatting with the other passengers, and then, **BLAM!** The limo hits a huge pothole and the passengers are jarred out of their belief in the pleasantness of the journey.

Some readers will momentarily balk, then continue with the story, forgiving the huge bump. Others will not: they will then or later simply stop reading the story because they feel they can't trust the author to continue with the story she implicitly promised.

Understanding point of view is important if you want to tell a story smoothly and convincingly. Employing the best point of view for the story you want to tell is also important, but I'll get to that later.

For some people, consistency of POV is very easy: these writers understand point of view and do not violate it. For others, point of view is a mystery. When somebody points out to them in which paragraph or which sentence they suddenly shifted points of view, they simply don't understand: they think the point of view is consistent. I have seen this happen often in writing classes and conferences.

First Person POV

Imagine that you, the writer, reside in a house high above the clouds, sort of like the giant in *Jack and the Beanstalk*. The characters you've created for your book reside far below you, on the ground. In order for you to tell your story, you lower a tiny, tiny camera on a super-thin filament down toward your characters.

If you lower that camera right into the head of one of your characters, say Frank Dragovic, you can see only what he sees, hear only what he hears, feel only what he feels. The camera is inside the mind of a single character, and you will tell the story from that character's point of view. This is called **first person POV**. To be exact, this is **first person singular POV**. The story is told from the viewpoint of a single character, usually (but not always) the protagonist.

But imagine that you want to lower more than one camera. Imagine you want to lower five cameras. If you lowered five different cameras into the heads of five different characters, then told the story from all five points of view, one at a time, alternating between characters, you would have **first person multiple POV**. The reader would experience the story from the first person POV of, say, Brian. Then Courtney. Then Jason. Then Vonda and, finally, Ulysses. And then the novel would continue, alternating among these characters in any order the author decides.

There's more. Suppose that you lowered those five cameras into the heads of five different characters, then told the story from their points of view, all at the same time. In this case you wouldn't have an "I" voice, you would have a "we" voice. *We did this. We did that. We feel this way.* This would be **first person plural POV** Although it's highly unusual (and risky) to write a novel from this point of view, it has been done, as in David Levithan's *Two Boys Kissing,* in which part of the story is told from the first person plural point of view. (Not only that: the narrators are dead.)

The first person singular POV has a long and noble tradition in mystery writing. Many private eye novels are written this way, as are many amateur detective novels. Thrillers and police procedurals tend to be written from the third person POV.

Below are four paragraphs from *Sound Proof,* which is first person singular point of view.

> I thought briefly of noncompliance — my gut reaction to cops ordering me around. But I realized that Mary Ployd was in deep trouble, the theft of instruments being little compared to the murder of a musician teaching at her festival. Murder, most likely, by one of the other festival participants.
> In working for Mary, I was working specifically to identify the instrument thief. But a substructure lurks beneath every specificity, and what I wasn't getting paid for — saving Mary's festival from ruin — was far more important than what I was getting paid for.
> If you could call it pay.
> Glancing out the window I noticed Suzanne walking toward the showers, a puzzled look on her face. She wore cargo shorts, a white tank top, and sandals. Her red hair hung loose. Coming here was probably a bad idea. No way were my actions convincing her she should move in with me. I wasn't there when she went to sleep, wasn't there when she woke up.

Third Person POV

Going back to the writer-in-the-sky analogy, you might not

want to lower your camera *into* the head of a character. You might prefer to lower it just *above* the head of a character, positioned so that it follows this person everywhere, knows what he or she sees, hears, thinks and feels. But the camera is not inside the head of the character, and because of this, the camera has a wider view. With the camera hovering just above the head of the POV character, the writer tells the story using the pronouns *he* or *she*, as in: *He walked into the pig sty and examined the fence. It didn't take him long to spot the problem.*

Below are the same four paragraphs from *Sound Proof,* but written from a third person point of view.

> Dragovic thought briefly of noncompliance — his gut reaction to cops ordering him around. But he realized that Mary Ployd was in deep trouble, the theft of instruments being little compared to the murder of a musician teaching at her festival. Murder, most likely, by one of the other festival participants.
> He knew that in working for Mary he was working specifically to identify the instrument thief. But he knew even more that a substructure lurked beneath every specificity, and what he wasn't getting paid for — saving Mary's festival from ruin — was far more important than what he was getting paid for.
> If, he thought ruefully, you could call it pay.
> Glancing out the window he noticed Suzanne walking toward the showers, a puzzled look on her face. She wore cargo shorts, a white tank top, and sandals. Her red hair hung loose. Dragovic realized that coming here was probably a bad idea. There was no way his actions could be convincing Suzanne that she should move in with him. He wasn't there when she went to sleep, he wasn't there when she woke up.

You can see that in the paragraphs above, the camera through which the story is told is not inside Frank Dragovic's skull. But it hovers very closely above him, following his every move and every thought. The story is being told from the **third person POV** or, in this case, **third person limited POV** — because the point of view is limited to a single character.

If you as the writer choose to lower not one camera to hover over one character, but, say, four cameras, each to hover over one of four characters, and you switched between these four cameras to tell the story, then you would be telling the story from **third person multiple POV.**

Here's an example from *She's on First,* which is told in third person multiple POV. The four characters from whose POV the story is told are T.M. Curry, Linda Sunshine, Neal Vanderlin, and Al Mowerinski. The first example below is from Curry's point of view, the second from Linda's.

> The batter popped a fly ball to right field. Easy out. The first two pitches to the next batter hit the ground in front of the plate. Curry winced. Fans, probably parents and other assorted relatives, had filled two short bleachers along first and third. Half had applauded the bouncing ball. The other half had screamed at the pitcher, telling him he ought to be taken out. The next two pitches were strikes. Chatter filled the infield and drifted back to Curry and Al. "Atta boy, Jimmy." "Good work." "Keep it up, Jimbo." "Easy out, Jimmy, easy out." "Swings like a rusty gate." "Won't even see it coming."
>
> The batter connected. A hard grounder. A symphony of clanging cowbells and screeching whistles filled the air. Saved by the shortstop, out at first. "Nice play." Sipping from the flask, Curry gave the shortstop his due. Not so half the fans, who shouted at the umpire who made the call, threatening to end his life.
>
> A strikeout retired the side. The other team took the field, their red and gray uniforms identifying them in block letters as the Warriors.
>
> The Fighters at bat performed an exercise in basic math: three up and three down. In the bottom of the second inning, the first Warrior batter hit a home run. 1-0. The Fighter coach strolled out to talk to his pitcher. "Leave him in," somebody shouted. "Take him out, coach — your son's a bum!" somebody answered. "Send him to the Peewees!" Spitting tobacco juice behind the mound, the coach talked to his son. Then, empty of saliva and advice, he strolled back to the bench.
>
> Curry observed that the next Warrior batter was the biggest of the bunch. An Al Mowerinski of the Little League, he must have been an old twelve, playing out his last summer, dwarfing the others, who looked like average ten-year-olds. The big kid took two balls and one strike, then smashed a line drive that caromed off the left

field fence. The miniature Warrior giant made it to second base. Could have made it to third if he'd been a hustler, Curry informed Al.

. . .

Linda, feeling dismissed and confused, twisted in her seat so that she faced away from Timothy Michael Curry.

When she looked his way again, he was reading the front section of his newspaper. She was so angry she didn't want to speak to him. But she realized that if she wanted to play baseball she had to deal with him — with him and hundreds like him. Clearing her throat, she asked for the sports section. With a heavy sigh, he separated it from the rest of the paper and handed it to her.

Okay, she told herself, forget this scout for the time being and read about baseball. She opened the sports section. The first thing that caught her eye was the headline, "Eagles Need Heart" The byline read "Neal Vanderlin." The photo that ran with the column pictured a man who could have written for the college paper: he looked young, confident, healthy. Gentle, though: not arrogant. Neal Vanderlin: had she heard of him before? No matter, she'd better pay attention to what he had to say about the Eagles.

As Linda read, the antagonism with Curry left her. Vanderlin was talking baseball, and talking it good. The new Chicago Eagles under Al Mowerinski were, he said, a body that wasn't completely built yet. *Great — Al Mowerinski's building a team!* Wally Szczpanozowski, the team's center fielder and slugger, was swinging wildly at any ball that looked round and white. Since all balls coming into the plate looked round and white, Zowski was doing a lot of swinging and hitting a lot of air. *Oh-oh. Was Zowski really that bad? Or did Vanderlin have a grudge against the Eagles?* Vanderlin complimented Harland Abilene, the young catcher just up from the minors, who showed he could take the pain, blocking dirt curves with his body. *Good.* It's too bad, Vanderlin pointed out, that the Eagles had so many pitchers who threw curves in the dirt. *Ouch*! Lacey Griffin, the third baseman, would be one of the all-time greats, as would Frank Laughing, the second baseman. *All right — a strong infield.* But Zack Weiss, the aging utility man who played shortstop for the Eagles, was not the person to cover the hole — he had already waved goodbye to an entire family reunion of Spaldings as they sped by him on their way to left field. *Jesus! What was with this Vanderlin?* Merle Isemonger, he wrote, was a big, strong pitcher who threw mighty hard. Once he could think mighty hard, he'd be what the Eagles needed to win. In short, concluded Vanderlin, the Eagles had a lot of body parts, but were missing a heart and a head.

Linda sat up. She looked at the photo of Vanderlin again. Had she thought he looked college? Had she thought he looked gentle? The photo lied. Either Vanderlin was waging a vendetta against every player on the Eagles, or, she supposed, this was the price you paid for playing in the majors. Making the majors meant more than batting, fielding, and base running: it meant becoming the butt of sportswriters. It meant having every error you made magnified and tele-typed across the country.

As you can see from these two excerpts, readers experience the story through different viewpoints, and each viewpoint is consistent with what that particular character believes. Third person limited POV is a common one for novels.

But say that you, sitting up there in your house in the clouds, think to yourself: *Hey, why limit myself to just a few cameras? I can lower fifty! I can lower one hundred! I can see into everybody and anybody's thoughts! Furthermore — I can supply my own observations on life, love, and everything else!*

If you decide to lower all those cameras to hover just above the heads of all the characters you create for your story, and if you switch among those characters anytime they are in a scene, *and* if you throw in your own thoughts as commentary or observation, you would be telling your story in the **third person omniscient POV**. Charles Dickens was a master of the omniscient point of view, which was very popular during the 19th century but is less popular in modern times. There has been a small revival of the omniscient point of view with books such as Kate DiCamillo's *The Tale of Despereaux*, written for middle grades. To me, third person omniscient has an old-fashioned feel to it. This doesn't mean it can't be used today: it might be the perfect point of view for the story you have in mind, especially if you want to set the story during the 19th century.

Second Person POV

This brings us to the final point of view, the **second person POV**. This is an atypical point of view, though short fiction of the last few decades has employed it. I've saved this for last because I can't immediately figure out how it fits into my camera analogy. In the second person point of view, either a single character in the novel or the narrator (somebody who is telling the story but is not a character in the novel — an unnamed entity) is speaking to the reader using the second person pronoun, *you*.

Here's how *Sound Proof* would sound if it were written in the second person.

> You think briefly of noncompliance — your gut reaction to cops ordering you around. But then you realize that Mary Ployd is in deep trouble, the theft of instruments being little compared to the murder of a musician teaching at her festival. Murder, most likely, by one of the other festival participants.
>
> In working for Mary, you are working specifically to identify the instrument thief. But you realize that a substructure lurks beneath every specificity, and what you aren't getting paid for — saving Mary's festival from ruin — is far more important than what you are getting paid for.
>
> If you could call it pay.
>
> Glancing out the window you notice Suzanne walking toward the showers, a puzzled look on her face. She's wearing cargo shorts, a white tank top, and sandals. Her red hair hangs loose. You realize that coming here was probably a bad idea. No way are your actions going to convince Suzanne that she should move in with you. You aren't there when she goes to sleep, you aren't there when she wakes up.

I once took a writing class which dealt with voice and point of view, and I remember the instructor stressing that the big problem with second person POV is that it could lose the reader in a heartbeat. In every place where the narrator says *you do this, you do that*, the reader might react with, *No, I do not!* — and slam the book closed. In fiction, people do not like being told what to do, and under certain circumstances they might not like being addressed as *you*, especially if the writing sounds as if it's the imperative voice (the voice which makes commands, as in *Stop!* which is really, *You stop!*).

And that brings me back to my camera analogy. In the second person voice, it's as if you, the author, have lowered the camera over the head of a character — but that character has grabbed the camera and twisted it back up at you. Or at the reader. The character is now in control and is telling readers what they're doing or how they're feeling. Few readers like this.

Those who argue in favor of second person point of view state that the voice is not commanding, that it comes directly from inside a character and is a way of trying to bring the character and the reader closer together, so that the two of them are "you." Some see it as a way of getting the reader more invested in the story.

First Person POV: Advantages and Disadvantages

Any point of view has both strengths and weaknesses, and it benefits you to understand what these strengths and weaknesses are before you plunge boldly into one or the other point of view. So let's examine the points of view again.

One of the greatest advantages of first person POV is its immediacy and the empathy it builds (usually) between the reader and the protagonist. We live our lives inside our own bodies and minds and we look at the world through our own eyes. We hear with our own ears and smell with our own noses. We *experience* through ourselves. And so, when we read a novel written from the first person POV, in which one person is experiencing the world, we can so easily identify with that "I" voice — because we live the "I" voice every moment of our lives.

With the first person POV, the reader senses that things are happening right away. And unless the character whose eyes we're experiencing the story through turns out to be totally unlikeable, the reader experiences empathy almost from the beginning. Immediacy and empathy are very important advantages of the first person POV.

The greatest disadvantage of the first person POV is that the writer must tell the story in such a way that the first person character is *always there*. Nothing can happen that the first person character doesn't see or hear. When you first start to write your novel, you may not think that first person POV is limiting — until you realize, some distance into the story, that you need to show the reader something that your first person narrator cannot have experienced. In such a case you might resort to having another character report to the main character . . . but such second-hand relaying of information will soon grow uninteresting. Some writers resort to suddenly shifting to a new point of view for just one crucial scene or chapter. Book reviewers usually comment on how jarring this is. I advise not doing it: such a blatant, temporary shift in point of view comes across as a mistake.

While I'm talking about first person POV, I want to digress a moment to mention that when you choose first person POV, your point-of-view character need not be the protagonist. In the case of *Dirty Proof* and *Sound Proof,* and in the case of most first-person novels, the viewpoint character and the protagonist are one and the same. But sometimes a writer chooses to make a secondary character the viewpoint, as did Nathaniel Hawthorne in *The Blithedale Romance* and as did F. Scott Fitzgerald in *The Great Gatsby.* As did Arthur Conan Doyle in the Sherlock Holmes stories.

Choosing a secondary character as the first-person narrator in a novel has two advantages. First, a secondary character can talk to other characters *about* the protagonist and *about* incidents. A secondary character can speculate on the motivations and actions of the protagonist — which a protagonist could not speculate on about himself! Also, a secondary character telling the story creates a sort of aesthetic distance from the protagonist, making the protagonist look larger than life. That's certainly the case in *The Blithedale Romance, The Great Gatsby,* and the Sherlock Holmes stories. Sherlock, as seen through Watson's eyes, is extraordinary in thought and action.

I believe that Hawthorne, Fitzgerald, and Doyle were very conscious of their choices and their reasons. In each case, I think the author wanted the reader to see the protagonist from the outside, not the inside, so that the protagonist would always remain something of a mystery. It's possible that **first person secondary-character POV** is the right POV for the story you want to tell.

Third Person POV: Advantages and Disadvantages

The third person limited POV is a very popular way of telling a story. The Harry Bosch novels by Michael Connelly are examples of this point of view. Harry is always referred to as *Bosch* by the writer, who tells us what Harry thinks and feels and notices. Third-person limited novels feel broader in scope than do first-person stories. That camera being outside the head of the character makes a huge difference in how a reader perceives what is happening. The third person limited POV of the Bosch novels conveys the feeling that the novels are about more than the individual case Harry is working on — they are more of a comment on society, criminals, the police, and our legal system. In third person point of view, the writing feels as if the narrator is telling the story with authority. Readers tend to not question the truthfulness of third person POV, whereas they more readily question the truthfulness of first person POV. Many a first person POV novel turns out to have an unreliable narrator: one who, as the story progresses, reveals that perhaps what he's telling us shouldn't be trusted. As mystery readers know, Dr. James Sheppard, first-person narrator of Agatha Christie's classic, *The Murder of Roger Ackroyd*, certainly can't be trusted.

The third person multiple POV is the choice of those who write blockbuster novels. Which isn't to say it can't be your choice, too, even if you aren't out to write a blockbuster novel. In *Writing the Blockbuster Novel*, author Albert Zuckerman (he is Ken Follett's agent) explains that a "big novel" is one which "involves the reader emotionally with more than one character." It does this through multiple points of view, *limited* to a few characters: three, four, or five. Zuckerman goes on to explain how Follett used this third person multiple POV in *The Man from St. Petersburg*, limiting it to four characters in the book.

Zuckerman argues that in order to write a blockbuster novel, a writer must learn how to use the third person multiple POV. He gives the example of John Grisham, whose first book, *A Time to Kill*, was written from something of an omniscient point of view, but whose top-ten novel, *The Firm*, was written from the third person multiple POV. Zuckerman believes that the author omniscient POV is a hindrance to developing reader empathy: "Readers, once they develop an interest in a few key characters, find it bothersome, frustrating even, to be brought again and again into the interiors of brand-new or distinctly minor characters, such as some of those in *A Time to Kill*."

In fact, third person multiple POV is an ideal method for telling many stories, whether or not they end up being blockbuster novels. As you saw earlier in this chapter, it's the method I chose for my first novel, *She's on First*, the story of a female major leaguer. I chose four characters from whose third-person points of view I told the story: Timothy Michael Curry is a baseball scout; Linda Sunshine is a baseball player; Al Mowerinski owns the major league Chicago Eagles; and Neal Vanderlin is a sports reporter. To use my writer-in-the-clouds analogy, I lowered four cameras and each hovered *above* (not *in*) the head of one of these four characters. I chose this method because it allowed me to tell a broader story than the story I could tell if I chose a first person POV.

Prepare the Reader

While third person multiple POV is the choice of many writers at all levels of experience, it is, I think, where writers make the most POV mistakes. One such mistake is writing from Character A's third-person POV for three chapters, say, then suddenly, in the fourth chapter, switching to a second main character's point of view. The reader is jarred. Worse yet, the reader is probably upset. He has entered a story thinking it's from the point of view of one and only one character. After fifty pages he learns otherwise! So when you use third person multiple POV, prepare the reader. Establish very early on that the story will be told from the POV of several characters. You can have the first chapter from the POV of one of those main characters, and the second chapter from the POV of another. The reader can handle that. It establishes a pattern.

Or you can introduce two of the main characters in the first chapter, and tell the story first from one's POV, then continue with the other's POV. When you do that, leave extra lines of white space between the ending of the first person's POV and the start of the second person's POV. Readers know what these lines of white space signal: a change in scene and/or a change in POV.

Remember that when writing from the third person multiple POV, you will have to choose *which* character your camera follows into each scene in the book. That character should be the one who has the most to lose or gain in the scene: the character who is most affected by the conflict present in that scene. Thus I chose Timothy Michael Curry as the first POV character in *She's on First*, in the college baseball game scene. Although Linda Sunshine is playing shortstop in the game, she's not the one who has the most to gain or lose, even if she knows that a major league scout is in the stands. Yes, she would *want* the scout to sign her to a major league contract, but if he doesn't there are other scouts and other major league teams. Curry, on the other hand, knows that if he signs Linda Sunshine, he will go down in history as the man who signed a woman to a major league contract. That is something Curry does *not* want on his record, and so, because he knows that he was sent to the game specifically to *sign* Sunshine, he has the most at stake in that particular conflict

As for the third person omniscient POV, it has, as you've read above, the distinct disadvantage of diluting rather than increasing reader identification with the story and the characters. However, third person omniscient might be the way you, the writer, see the story, and if you're convinced that's the right way to tell the story you have in mind, then do it.

How You See the Story

In fact, the way *you* see the story has much to do with the point of view you choose. Many books on writing imply that there is a *right* point of view for each individual novel. That's sort of true, and sort of not true — because if you wrote a novel first in one point of view, then rewrote it in a different point of view, it would be a different story. The characters would be the same and the plot would be the same. But the reader experience of the story — that sense of not only plot, characters, and setting, but the sense of perspective (an attitude toward the story) —would be different.

A Harry Bosch story told from the first person POV wouldn't have the same broader view that the third person POV gives the story.

If I had written *Sound Proof* from the third person POV rather than the first, most of the humor would be lost, because so much of the humor comes from the difference between the music festival as participants see it and the way Frank, an outsider, sees it.

Sometimes your gut instinct tells you the best POV for your story. Other times you end up thinking long and hard, and experimenting, before you come up with the right POV. I've been in writing classes (as a student) and in critique sessions, and I know from these experiences that sometimes (perhaps as much as 10-20% of the time) the initial POV a writer chooses isn't the best for the story she or he wants to tell. This becomes evident when readers or critique group members start asking questions about how and why things take place. Sometimes a change in point of view can make a dramatic difference to the story you want to tell. So changing POV is very worth considering. It means you need to see the story in a new way: a way that allows you to do things the story needs.

I've written scores of books for children and for adults, and I can recall changing POV only once. I had originally told the story (through many rewrites) in third person limited POV. Nobody said that I should change this. The story was a picture book, and almost all picture books are told in one form or another of third person POV. But somehow, during my rewrites, I sensed that the POV was impeding my telling of the story.

It's a story about my father's childhood in a small mountain village in Croatia. It's a story he told me, on and off, over the years. One day as I was looking at the manuscript, I suddenly saw the whole thing in the "I" voice — because that's how my father told it to me. And so I rewrote (again, several times) with a totally different point of view. And although first person POV is highly unusual for a picture book, it's not unheard of. And, in my opinion, it makes a much better story in this particular case.

Don't Violate Point of View

In conclusion, choosing point of view is difficult for some

writers, easy for others. Some instinctively "see" how the story they have in mind is best told. Others experiment, perhaps writing the first three chapters in one POV, then rewriting them in another, to see which POV coincides with their writer's vision.

There is no right or wrong point of view (not even second person or author omniscient) as such. But there could be in some cases a "better" point of view for the story you want to tell. If you sense there's a better point of view for your story than the one you've chosen, strive to find that better point of view through experimentation.

Whichever POV you choose, one cardinal rule applies: *be consistent!* Don't violate point of view: don't jar readers. If you're writing in first person POV, you cannot tell us something that happens when the POV character isn't present. Readers will hate you for this inconsistency. If you're writing in third person multiple, you cannot suddenly tell us what another character (not one of your chosen few) is thinking. That is a violation of point of view, and readers will be jarred out of their pleasant reading experience.

Here's an example of violation of point of view, from one of the *She's on First* passages previously quoted.

> Linda, feeling dismissed and confused, twisted in her seat so that she faced away from Timothy Michael Curry.
> When she looked his way again, <u>Curry was considering calling Al, telling him the deal was off, he didn't recommend Sunshine. Not now, not ever.</u>
> She was so angry she didn't want to speak to him. But she realized that if she wanted to play baseball she had to deal with him — with him and hundreds like him. Clearing her throat, she asked for the sports section. <u>Wishing she could just disappear, vanish like a towering home run, never to be retrieved, Curry separated the sports section from the rest of the paper and handed it to her.</u>
> Okay, she told herself, forget this scout for the time being and read about baseball. She opened the sports section. The first thing that caught her eye was the headline, "Eagles Need Heart" The byline read "Neal Vanderlin." The photo that ran with the column pictured a man who could have written for the college paper: he

looked young, confident, healthy. Gentle, though: not arrogant. Neal Vanderlin: had she heard of him before? No matter, she'd better pay attention to what he had to say about the Eagles.

The two underlined sentences are a violation of point of view (unless the point of view is author omniscient: which in this case it isn't). In this section of the novel, the camera is hovering over the head of Linda Sunshine, reporting what she does and what she thinks and feels. But in the underlined sentences, the camera is *not* over her head: it is over the head of T.M. Curry, reflecting what *he* thinks and feels. The camera has jumped from one character to another in a section in which it should remain steady and true.

The jolt in point of view disrupts the reading experience. It's your job as writer to make that reading experience as pleasant as possible.

9 Summary, Scene, and Conflict

Novels are built through a series of scenes. These scenes are part of the plot and are thus connected by cause and effect. Plays are also built through a series of scenes. In fact, plays are all scene: dialogue and action in real time. Novels, however, are built not only through scenes, but also through summary or, as it's also called, narrative summary, or simply narrative. While on-stage drama has the power of scenes, novels have not only that power, but the additional breadth and depth that narrative summary gives. There's a slant or stand in novels that doesn't exist in plays: that slant comes through the narrative. (Throughout this book I'll use *summary* and *narrative* interchangeably.) The choice every novelist makes when writing is: Should I tell this part of the story in scene, or should I tell it in summary?

Conflict

A scene is a dramatic incident that takes place in real time, without interruption, usually in the same place. It usually involves two or more characters, it usually involves dialogue, and it always involves conflict. Always.

In writing classes and in critique groups I've found, to my initial surprise, that many people are averse to conflict. It appears they don't want people, even their own characters, to disagree. As a result of this learned aversion to conflict, these people either write boring scenes or they avoid scenes altogether and write mostly narrative summary.

When culture-instillers teach children that conflict is bad, they're doing it partly to protect the child from repercussions and partly to protect society from a person who insists on asserting his will at all times. But conflict, which is the lifeblood of scene, is present in every aspect of our lives.

That conflict can be minor. What do I wear to work today? I'm sick and tired of oatmeal for breakfast, let's have bacon and eggs! Should I shovel the front sidewalk now, or after I get home from work? Why am I always seated next to Zack, who bores me to death? We've never taken a mountain vacation — should we skip the beach this year and try the mountains?

Or it can be major. Do we form a union to fight for our jobs and health benefits? Should we invest our savings in real estate or an IRA? What should I do about this man who's been following me for blocks? Either your brother finds his own place in the next two weeks, or I move out!

Conflict is part of life, from the moment we're born until the moment we die. Infants might want food, but can't express themselves: they are experiencing the conflict of wanting something but not getting it. Adults might know they need eight hours of sleep for good health and optimum performance, but at the same time they want to stay up late to watch a movie. Conflict, conflict, conflict.

Conflict can be good, bad, or even neutral, depending on the situation and the people involved. Whether you have oatmeal instead of bacon and eggs for breakfast could be a totally neutral conflict if you enjoy both meals and just can't decide between them. If your partner has been making you oatmeal for breakfast for the last two weeks and, despite your requests, will not stop serving you oatmeal, that could be a very bad conflict — one that might get worse as each of you expresses your wants.

The purpose of all the information about conflict is this: every scene must have a conflict, either small, medium, or large. Either good, neutral, or bad. Either explicit or implicit. If you write scenes that have no conflict, you will be writing scenes for no purpose. The reader will become bored.

The Purpose of Scene

The purpose of scene is to advance the plot and help develop characterization. Both of these are accomplished through conflict. Here's a scene from *Sound Proof*. It takes place the morning after the murder and after the sheriff has questioned Frank. The scene takes place at breakfast in the community dining hall.

> Nola Grayson, sitting with Suzanne and me, added sugar and cream to her coffee, stirred it, and settled the spoon alongside the cup. "Mary and I have talked about Shelby's death," she said, "and while it is tragic that somebody has died at Midwest Music Madness, it's important for the festival to continue in the spirit intended. A spirit of fun, relaxation, friendship. And good music."
>
> I nodded absentmindedly, wondering if I had missed any clue . . . Bliss smelling of cigarette smoke, Edric English fully dressed, the cut strings twisted around the red fiddle. . . .
>
> ". . . do you agree?" Nola asked.
>
> Suzanne prodded my thigh.
>
> "Huh? Agree with what?"
>
> "That we want the festival to be a positive experience for everybody, so we should proceed like we usually do."
>
> "Sure," I said.
>
> Nola nodded. "Good. That's what I told Aja, and so she wants to talk to you."
>
> I stared blankly at Nola. "Aja Freeman?" I asked. "One of the cooks?"
>
> "*Yes,*" said Nola in exasperation.
>
> "What about?" I asked.
>
> Nola smiled and leaned forward as if we were conspiring. "Aja *really* wants to win the cooking contest this year, and she's got it into her head that more table space will help. Do you think you can build a table for the kitchen staff?"
>
> Build a table. I thought about it for a long minute.
>
> "Sure," I said at last. "That's what I'm here for," I lied, wondering if Mary had carpentry work planned for me every day. "I'll talk to Aja this morning."

The conflict in this scene is not a large one, certainly not as large as other scenes in the book (Frank's discovery of the body, the scene in which Frank discovers the blackmail note, the storm scene, the confrontation between Mary and Raven, and so on). Nevertheless, there *is* a conflict, and the scene does advance the plot and help characterize.

Nola Grayson wants Frank to build a table for the kitchen staff (Frank is still working undercover as a carpenter), but his mind is not even on the conversation: he's analyzing what he observed just a few hours ago when he discovered Stubbs' body. Nola wants Frank to build a table, Frank wants to solve the crime. This is the conflict. Despite what he wants to do (figure out who murdered Shelby Stubbs), Frank decides to continue his undercover role as carpenter. This reveals something about Frank's character: he takes his job seriously and so he continues working undercover. And he takes murder seriously, whether it's his job or not.

Nola's character is also developed in this scene: she takes the running of Mary's festival seriously. Despite the murder, she wants things to continue as "normal," and so she focuses on a very normal thing, the building of a needed table for the kitchen staff.

Suzanne's character is also developed in this scene. She is sitting next to Frank, and when it's clear to her that he has lost the thread of the conversation, she prods his thigh, a motion that most likely goes undetected at the long community tables. Suzanne doesn't want Frank to look inattentive, so she brings him back to the conversation at hand. But she doesn't do it by calling attention to his lapse ... by saying something like, "Frank. Nola's speaking to you." Suzanne is helping Frank look good.

The scene above could be written without any conflict. Here's what it might look like:

> Nola Grayson, sitting with Suzanne and me, added sugar and cream to her coffee, stirred it, and settled the spoon alongside the cup. "Mary and I have talked about Shelby's death," she said, "and while it is tragic that somebody has died at Midwest Music Madness, it's important for the festival to continue in the spirit intended. A spirit of fun, relaxation, friendship. And good music."
> "Yes," I replied, agreeing wholeheartedly.
> "We want the festival to be a positive experience for everybody, so we should proceed like we usually do," Nola continued.
> "That makes sense," I said.
> Nola nodded. "Good. That's what I told Aja, and

> so she wants to talk to you."
> "What about?" I asked.
> Nola smiled and leaned forward as if we were conspiring. "Aja *really* wants to win the cooking contest this year, and she's got it into her head that more table space will help. Do you think you can build a table for the kitchen staff?"
> "Sure," I said. "I'll talk to Aja right after breakfast."

I hope you aren't enamored of the above scene, because it's totally uninteresting. There's no conflict at all. Because there's no conflict, the scene doesn't move the plot forward. Nor does it help characterize anybody.

If No Conflict, Then Summarize

If you find yourself writing bland scenes which contain no conflict, you can improve your story in one of two ways. If you sense that the scene is important to your story, then rewrite the scene so that it contains conflict and helps reveal character. Or, drop the scene and relay the information as narrative summary.

Here's what my scene might look like in narrative summary:

> At breakfast Nola Grayson sat with Suzanne and me, mainly to inform me that she and Mary had talked over the murder and its ramifications for the festival, and that they both felt the festival should continue in the spirit intended.
> Part of me listened to what Nola was saying. But only a small part. The larger part of my brain was occupied with whether I had missed any clues last night . . . Bliss smelling of cigarette smoke, Edric English fully dressed, the cut strings twisted around the red fiddle. . . .
> When Nola got my attention again, she asked me to build a table for the kitchen staff. I thought about it and realized that working undercover as a carpenter might be helping the theft investigation. But it sure as hell wasn't helping the murder investigation — not if I had to spend time pounding together a table when I should be asking questions.

This narrative summary isn't, in my opinion, as interesting as the scene was. But it's perfectly acceptable as summary, and it does move the story forward. A choice that you as a writer will always be making is this: what to tell in scene, what to tell in summary. Sometimes your decision will be the correct one either way. This is especially true when not much is at stake.

If you find yourself presenting most of your book in narrative summary, however, you need to reconsider your choice. Why are you choosing narrative summary, which avoids direct action and conflict, and instead tells the story in a second-hand manner? Readers crave drama, so it's up to you to give them the important parts of your story through scenes. It's up to you to decide what those scenes are.

Conflict Without Dialogue

Earlier in this chapter I said of scene: "It usually involves two or more characters, it usually involves dialogue, and it always involves conflict. Always."

You may wonder whether a scene can be built with perhaps only one character and no dialogue. Such scenes aren't common, but they do exist, and there's a time and place for them. Below is part of the long storm-rescue scene from chapter eighteen of *Sound Proof*. Frank has just stepped out of the barn and into the fierce storm in order to find and save Lafayette Wafer, who was last seen at the pole barn, which lies across the creek from the main barn.

> The first four steps weren't that bad. Like stepping into a pugnacious, overweight waterfall. After that the wind whipped around the corner of the barn and bulldozed me in directions I didn't want to go. But mostly it came from the west and I was heading east, so for a while it simply impelled me forward.
> Coming back would be the problem.
> Even with the powerful flashlight in my hand, the path wasn't visible. Walls of water poured down, obscuring everything. I tried to run but couldn't, the wind shoving me everywhere. I fell, got up, was blown back down a couple of times. Being blown off my feet didn't bother me too much, at least not yet. What made my heart

race harder was the fear of lightning. It crackled in the sky behind me as if deciding where to aim next.

Uncle Rudy's thunderstorm advice filled my brain. When out in the fields during a thunderstorm, never go near a tall tree that could attract lightning. Never stand upright. Never lie flat. Instead, crouch: present the smallest surface possible to the bolts from above. My sister and cousins and I would go around pretending we were running from lighting, our backs curved, our arms hanging loosely at our sides. We'd sway back and forth and huff-huff like apes.

Back then, it was funny.

Now it was damned awkward to run all hunched over, as close to the ground as possible.

The one-pound pork chop I had eaten cramped my stomach, making progress even more difficult. If I survived, I would not vote for Tansy Thompson as best cook.

The wind knocked me over again and I fought my way back up, trying to remember which direction I'd been heading. I chose what I thought was the right one, then looked back over my shoulder. At that moment Guy must have rolled the barn door open — a huge rectangle of light shown through the darkness. I turned my back on it, confident of my bearing.

Several minutes later I sensed something massive, as if it were sending out vibrations. I looked up. The black walnut tree loomed, its branches whipsawing in the wind, its trunk swaying. The pole barn, then, was to my left.

I veered in that direction. I sloshed through the swift creek, forgetting to crouch as I hurried against the rising water, which had already reached the pole barn. I clicked the flashlight button: a long beam of light picked up the barn wall. The door wouldn't slide open. I pulled and pushed and at last squeezed through an opening.

"Lafayette!" I shouted.

He stood in the far corner . . . on the little ladder nailed to the wall, his bowed psaltry case clutched to his chest.

The storm-rescue scene is one of the longer ones in the book: this excerpt represents only part of it. The paragraphs are here to show, first, that this is a scene, even though it does not, until the last two paragraphs, contain dialogue or even two characters.

So what makes this a scene and not narrative summary?

First, it contains action. Second, that action is taking place as the scene progresses — in real time, not in summary. (Even though the story is told in the past tense, which is the most common way of writing fiction, the action is understood to be taking place as Frank relates it.) Conflict dominates the scene, even though it's not conflict between two or more people. Instead, it's conflict between a person and nature. Frank wants to make his way through the storm to the pole barn to bring Lafayette back to safety. Nature, always indifferent to humans, makes no accommodations to Frank's wishes. He and nature are in conflict. The storm is his obstacle. It will not back down or go away.

Some scenes can end in a stalemate. When that happens in a novel, the conflict will arise again, later in the book. Perhaps several more times, until the conflict is resolved one way or the other. But most scenes cannot end in a stalemate. The storm scene cannot. Either Frank will find Lafayette and bring him back, or the storm will prevent him from doing that. Either Frank "wins" or the storm "wins."

A book is created through a combination of scene and summary. The relationship between the two varies the rhythm and pace of the story. If you've just written a scene full of heavy conflict and intense stakes, the reader (and you!) could use the break of narrative summary before encountering another scene.

Determining which events to write as scene and which as summary is a learning experience. Even experienced novelists turn some scenes into summary during their rewrites, and some summaries into scenes. You, too, will consider these possibilities when you rewrite the first draft of your novel.

Subplots

It may be possible to write a novel that has no subplots. There would be one and only one story, and by default it would be the main story. There would be no other stories within the novel than the main story. Chances are this would be a dull book.

Why? Because subplots exist in almost all novels, where they function in several different ways:

- **to provide relief from the main plot, be it comic relief or just plain diversion**
- **to reveal backstory**
- **to aid in characterization**
- **to provide parallels or contrasts and thus enrich the theme**

How Many Subplots?

As its name implies, a subplot is a secondary plot in a work of fiction, its importance being less than that of the main plot. Like plots, subplots have their own plot points and rising action. Their story is sometimes parallel to the main story, sometimes intertwined with it. Some writing teachers say that a subplot should contain either different characters from the main plot, or occur at a different location, or take place at a different time. I don't agree with this 100% of the time, particularly when it comes to mystery novels, where the plots and subplots are often intertwined.

How many subplots a novel contains is up to the writer and the story he wants to tell, but keep in mind that an adult novel probably requires at least two subplots in order to maintain reader interest and expand the story's scope, but perhaps no more than five subplots, else the main plot might seem less important. (I've read novels which have seven or eight or nine subplots and find that the multitude of subplots lessens the intensity of my experience with the main plot.)

The subplots should come to the fore just often enough for relief and to keep them fresh in the readers' minds, but not so often that they interfere with the main plot. Whether your subplots are separate (in characters, location, or time) or intertwined, they need to be scattered throughout your novel in a planned way. If you have three subplots you would of course introduce A first, then B, then C. But you need not continue in that order — readers would soon pick up on the rigid order and become bored, or at least lose their sense of anticipation. You could change the order to something like this: A B C B C A C B B A C. Or some other order.

In *Building Better Plots* Robert Kernen advises using notecards to build and lay out plots and subplots. He suggests using a different color of notecard for each subplot. So if your main plot notecards are white, subplot A could be written on pink cards, subplot B on green cards, and subplot C on yellow cards. Kernen advocates spreading the notecards on a large table, then moving them around to figure out not only the order of events for the main plot, but also to figure out where to begin, continue, and end the subplots.

If you find that you have seven plot points for subplot A, and you find that you have seven pink notecards all bunched together on the table, this could be a sign telling you to rethink the structure of your novel. Do you really want to introduce and conclude subplot A in one area of the novel? Maybe that's necessary, in which case the answer is *Yes, I do*. But maybe it's not necessary, in which case the answer might be, *Hmmm: I think I'll move some of these pink notecards to the center, and some nearer the end.*

Because each subplot is a story, it needs conflict, rising action, and resolution. I've already talked about conflict in a previous chapter, and I'll talk about rising action in a later one. That leaves resolution — the solving of a problem or situation. Readers feel greater satisfaction when the issues in a story are resolved. Sometimes readers feel great impatience and disappointment if the issues are *not* resolved. In most cases, the subplots you introduce to your story need to be resolved. That resolution can either be spelled out in detail *or* very strongly suggested. (The resolution of my Mary-and-the-Sheriff subplot is strongly suggested.)

When it comes to series, though, many authors choose to not resolve certain subplots, but rather to carry them over from one book to the next. And the next. Subplots such as: will the hero stop drinking? will the protagonist and his love interest break apart? or get together? what will happen to the main character's sister, who seems on the verge of a bad marriage? And so on.

As both a reader and a writer, I think it's fine to have one or two subplots that aren't resolved until the next book in the series. Or perhaps the book after that one. But as a reader, I become extremely annoyed if it appears that a subplot is being dragged on forever, one book after another after another. When you write your mystery, keep in mind whether or not, and when, to resolve each of your subplots.

Subplots and Third Person POV

How you present your subplots to the reader is largely determined by the point of view you've chosen for your novel. If you've chosen to tell your story in **third person limited POV**, as many mystery and espionage writers do, you will most likely signal your subplots by the use of white space on the page — white space that separates what came before from what comes now, in terms of time, characters, or location. Michael Connelly and many, many other mystery writers use this time-honored technique to indicate that while the POV is still the same (Harry Bosch, third person limited POV), the time, place, or characters with Harry have changed. Readers have no difficulty following what is happening: the white space prepares them.

On the other hand, if you've chosen **third person multiple POV** to tell your story (as I did with *She's on First*), you could also use white space to switch between the characters and the stories. Some of the characters you choose for third person multiple POV will of necessity be part of a subplot that interweaves with the main plot: it's very difficult to write a story with four POVs, say, in which all four characters are protagonists. Not impossible. But definitely difficult.

If you're telling your story in **third person multiple POV** in alternating chapters, one for each character whose POV you depict, then the telling and placement of your subplots will be determined by which character they belong to. If one of the POV characters is Travis, and his story is a subplot, then that subplot will appear in the chapters from Travis's POV — or possibly in chapters from other characters' POVs when they're interacting with Travis. In third person multiple POV told in alternating chapters, there would not be a strong reason to signal a subplot by the use of white space on the page. But it would still be possible to do this if you needed to.

Subplots and First Person POV

If you've chosen to tell your story from the **first person singular POV**, as I told *Sound Proof,* then you cannot separate the subplots from the POV (as you could with third person limited and third person multiple POV). The entire story will be seen from the eyes of your sole POV character, and so she will be present at every incident in the story, including the subplots. Of course the location could change, the time could change, and the characters (except for the POV character) could change each time one of the subplots appears.

Weaving the subplots into a first person POV story is a bit trickier than weaving them into either of the other POVs — all because your POV character is always there. This isn't to say that you can't use the white space technique in a first person POV novel. You certainly can, and it will serve the same function as it does in the other POVS: signaling a change in time, place, or characters. I've read first person POV stories in which this is done.

With first person POV, though, I prefer a smoother reading experience than the bumps of white spaces allow. So in plotting *Sound Proof* I integrated my subplots into the main plot without much use of white space. (I used chapter breaks much more than I used white space.) If you choose to write from the first person POV, you may end up doing the same. But the other guidelines for developing subplots still apply: scatter them throughout the story;

be sure they contribute to the main plot or provide contrast to the main plot; be sure they develop and reveal character.

Subplots in *Sound Proof*

In *Sound Proof* there are many characters; there's theft, blackmail, and murder; there's the music; the instruments; the farm. There's the main plot. And there are four subplots:

> (A) the story of Frank and Suzanne's relationship: will she move in with him?
> (B) the story of Mary and the guitar she intentionally leaves on the stoop each day
> (C) the story of Mary and Yale's relationship: what went wrong and why
> (D) the story of Mary and the blackmail notes

For now, let's look at how I scattered these subplots throughout the 28-chapter novel, and whether or not I resolved them.

Chapter	Main Plot	Subplots
1	Frank Dragovic starts his investigation at Midwest Music Madness	Frank and Suzanne
2	Frank inspects festival grounds	Frank and Suzanne
3	Frank considers additional suspects	Frank and Suzanne Mary and Guitar
4	Frank questions Lafayette Frank takes drumming class	
5	An instrument is stolen, Frank questions people Frank's hammer is stolen	Frank and Suzanne
6	Frank attends dance with others, Patrols grounds at night	Frank and Suzanne
7	Frank hears moaning, investigates, discovers Stubbs body, bludgeoned to death	Sheriff and Mary

Chapter	Main Plot	Subplots
8	Frank searches for Lafayette	Frank and Suzanne
9	Frank questions those who had access to his hammer	
10	Frank questions Mary about a previous festival death	Mary and Guitar Sheriff and Mary Mary and Blackmail
11	Frank and Sheriff discuss motivations for murder	Frank and Suzanne
12	Frank observes Guy Dufour and later patrols the grounds at night	Frank and Suzanne Sheriff and Mary Mary and Blackmail
13	Sheriff shares some thoughts with Frank	Sheriff and Mary
14	Frank observes suspects during lunch A stolen instrument is recovered	Frank and Suzanne
15	Sheriff suspects Frank of the murder	Sheriff and Mary Frank and Suzanne
16	Frank searches farmhouse rooms Frank finds stolen fiddle	
17	Major storm hits the area Frank questions Edric	
18	All attendees run to barn for shelter Frank goes out to find Lafayette	Frank and Suzanne
19	Frank finds the stolen hurdy-gurdy	Sheriff and Mary Mary and Blackmail
20	Frank waits for the blackmailer, who is caught Murder weapon is found: it is Frank's hammer	Mary and Blackmail: **RESOLVED** Sheriff and Mary
21	Sheriff takes Frank to town for questioning Nola Grayson, attorney, accompanies Frank	
22	Frank follows police back to festival Mary either falls or is pushed from the hayloft door She survives	Sheriff and Mary Frank and Suzanne Mary and Guitar

Chapter	Main Plot	Subplots
23	Nola tells Frank that Mary left a document to be opened only after her death	Sheriff and Mary Mary and Guitar: **RESOLVED**
24	Another instrument is stolen	Frank and Suzanne
25	Frank finds the stolen instruments, enlists the Sheriff's help	Sheriff and Mary
26	Frank gives Mary instructions about the evening's final musical performance Frank and the Sheriff apprehend the instrument thief	Frank and Suzanne
27	Frank returns the stolen fiddle to Mary Frank confronts Mary about what she has been hiding	Sheriff and Mary
28	Frank stops the murderer from killing Mary	Sheriff and Mary: **RESOLVED** Frank and Suzanne

As you can see, Subplot A, the relationship between Frank and Suzanne, is the subplot that is present most often, appearing in fourteen of the twenty-eight chapters. This seems reasonable in that Frank is the protagonist and Suzanne is his love interest, and she's the reason he's at Midwest Music Madness. This subplot is not resolved. (But I promise to not carry it over forever!)

Subplot B, the story of Mary and the guitar she leaves on the stoop each day, is introduced in chapter three and resolved in chapter twenty-three. It's present in only four of the twenty-eight chapters.

Subplot C, the story of the Sheriff and Mary, is introduced in chapter seven and resolved in chapter twenty-eight. It's present in twelve of the twenty-eight chapters.

Subplot D, the story of Mary and the blackmail notes, is introduced in chapter ten and resolved in chapter twenty. It's present in four of the twenty-eight chapters.

You can see that I have two subplots that span most of the novel, and two that are contained within the central portion of the novel only. In other words, two long subplots and two short subplots. I could have had four long subplots, which might have been satisfying. Four short ones would not have been satisfying to readers, who enjoy subplots and don't necessarily want to see each and every one of them short and sweet.

I didn't follow Robert Kernen's suggestion that the subplots be resolved in the order they're introduced, each of them tied off before the novel's climax. Two of my subplots (A and C) continue on into the denouement. I further veered from Kernen's suggestions in that B is resolved not before D, but after D. For the purposes of the mystery (introducing possible motives in both the main plot and subplots), my subplot order works. Each introduces new suspicions and a new line of investigation and is then resolved as the detective eliminates possibilities, narrowing the hunt to the one actuality.

You need subplots in your mystery, so as you think about your main plot, think also about subplots. Consider that some of them can relate directly to the mystery, probably complicating it and leading the detective and/or the reader down the path of false clues. Consider also that some of them can probably *not* relate to the mystery, if only for relief from the mystery itself. For the most part, the subplot of Frank and Suzanne's relationship doesn't relate to the mystery itself.

And remember that your subplots, like your scenes, should contain conflict and reveal character.

11 Plot Complications

In a mystery you want plot complications — occurrences or discoveries that serve to make the story more complicated (until the resolution). You don't want so many plot complications that the reader is left saying, *What?* when she finishes the novel. Nor so few that the pace is slow and the conclusions obvious.

A subplot, you will recall, is a story within a story, and your mystery will probably have from two to five subplots. Subplots may serve as complications, the way the romance between Mary and the Sheriff does in *Sound Proof*. But they don't have to be complications. They can run parallel to the mystery and not complicate it at all, the way the romance between Frank and Suzanne does.

Unlike a subplot, a complication is not a story with its own beginning, middle, and end, with its own characters and conflicts. Instead, a complication is a new circumstance that the protagonist must deal with in the course of solving the mystery. Sometimes the complication will lead the detective astray: the detective thinks the complication is important to the solution of the mystery, and follows the complication — but as it turns out, the complication has nothing to do with the solution to the crime. So the detective must return to the mystery.

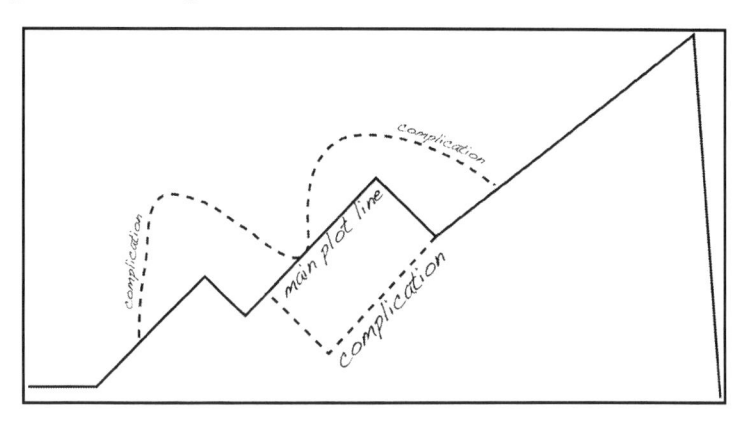

Examine the graphic example of what one, two, or three complications might look like. In each case, the "solution" of the complication leads the protagonist back to the main plot line.

In some cases plot complications arise directly out of characters and their situations. You'll find yourself writing a chapter when all of a sudden an insight comes to you and you write something other than what you had originally intended. That could be your subconscious speaking to you through your characters. You don't plan these plot complications: they happen spontaneously, just like Richard, the pig, happened spontaneously as I was writing *Sound Proof*.

Other plot complications will be those that you plan in advance, as you're outlining your novel. Or, if you don't outline, then as you're thinking about or working on your novel. In writing *Sound Proof* I planned most of my plot complications in advance. On exception is the relationship between Edric and Bliss, which came to me as I was writing, not before.

Some of your plot complications will serve to introduce red herring clues and/or to throw suspicion on different characters. Complications may block off or end one line of investigation, thus causing the detective to pursue another.

As with subplots, it's common to introduce your plot complications one by one and resolve them one by one. In whatever order you introduce and resolve them, these complications are more satisfying if they contribute to both the *advancement of the plot* and to the *deepening of the mystery* for the reader. (For the detective, too, but the detective is usually smarter than the reader and so will not be confused by some of the complications that stymie the reader.)

Detectives and Readers Are Intelligent

Remember this about plot complications: people who solve mysteries are intelligent in several different ways. They notice things. They draw inferences from what they observe. They think in terms of cause and effect. They understand motivation. They have sharp minds which, when it comes to drawing logical conclusions, are sharper than the minds of most people.

Therefore don't make a mistake so commonly made by some mystery writers — do *not* let your protagonist appear to be stupid when it comes to observing, understanding, or inferring. A less-than-sharp detective could be a real turn off to an intelligent reader. If you want to have your protagonist overlook something or fail to draw the correct inference, you need to work hard to make this believable to the reader. Coming up with a reason or situation in which your protagonist fails to notice or draw the correct conclusion about a clue may take days or weeks of your time. But the time spent will be worth it. You will be playing fair not only with the reader, but also with your protagonist.

Examples of Plot Complications

In *Sound Proof* the first plot complication comes in chapter two, where Frank notices that Edric English watches Shelby Stubbs and Bliss Beckins "like a hawk." When the hurdy-gurdy is stolen, Edric is in Stubbs' RV with Bliss. Still later, when Stubbs' body is discovered, Edric comes to see what the problem is, notices the body, and leaves immediately. The relationship between Stubbs, Edric, and Bliss is a plot complication. It doesn't appear to be related to the instrument thefts: neither Stubbs nor Edric nor Bliss were present the two previous years when instruments were stolen. But it could be related to the murder.

As the detective, Frank Dragovic has to decide whether this plot complication is related to the theft and/or murder. And if so, how. As a law enforcement officer, the Sheriff has to ask himself the same questions, and when he learns that Edric English served prison time for theft eighteen years earlier, he puts Edric high on the list of murder suspects. In the last chapters of the book the Sheriff is still pursuing the Edric-Bliss relationship as a possible motive for murder, but Frank has already figured out the meaning of the complication and eliminated Bliss and Edric from the list of murder suspects.

Another plot complication is introduced in chapter five, when Frank's hammer is either borrowed or stolen. (Frank abandons his tool belt in the drumming class when he races to answer the distressed cries of Guy Dufour.) After he realizes his hammer has been stolen, Frank spends some time trying to track it down. He questions Raven, who had used a hammer earlier. He questions Jeff Glover, who says that Guy Dufour borrowed a hammer. He questions Guy. He looks in various places where somebody may have mislaid or hidden a hammer.

Frank is very bothered by this complication for two reasons. First, the hammer is one that his father gave him when he was sixteen years old. Two, after Frank finds Stubbs' bludgeoned-to-death body, he realizes that a hammer may have been the weapon used. And he wonders if somebody stole his hammer in order to murder Stubbs. Much later in the novel, Frank's hammer is found, and it was, indeed, the murder weapon. Raven's confession not only clears up the missing-murder-weapon complication, but also the missing-fiddle-case complication.

When it comes to mystery novels, readers love plot complications, both because complications add spice to the mixture and because such complications allow readers to pit their skills against those of the protagonist. As I said earlier, not all of these plot complications need to be related to the mystery, but they should *appear* to be related — otherwise they aren't complicating anything. The relationship between Edric and Bliss appears to be related to the murder of Shelby Stubbs, but in fact is not. Nevertheless, readers find the explanation very satisfying: they went through the experience of wondering if Edric and/or Bliss were the murderers, and they are happy with the resolution.

The complication of the stolen hammer *is* directly related to the murder. Readers would probably find it disappointing if there were an innocent reason for the hammer's disappearance. I know that as a reader I often find "innocent explanations" disappointing in mysteries. They feel like a letdown of my expectations.

Furthermore, the complication of the stolen hammer, once the hammer is found and determined to be the murder weapon, helps Frank work toward a solution. He knows who could *not* have stolen his hammer — Guy Dufour, for one, who was screaming about his stolen hurdy-gurdy and within Frank's sight the entire time. Fonnie Sheffler and Vance Jurasek, for two more, because they were where the hurdy-gurdy was stolen and nowhere near the drumming class. And he knows who had the opportunity to steal his hammer: Cody Thompson, Kim Oberfeld, Jeff Glover, Lafayette Wafer, and Kofi Quay. Because the hammer theft enables Frank to narrow down the list of murder suspects, it serves to advance the plot.

Also, the complication serves to develop character: it tells us the murder was premeditated, and it shows us that Raven is so concerned for herself that she's willing to tamper with evidence at the scene of the crime *and* willing to use that evidence to implicate Mary Ployd.

When writing your mystery novel, add plot complications in order to make your detective work harder, in order to satisfy readers, and in order to enrich the story.

Casting Suspicion

Just as fishermen cast a net to spread over a large area and gather the fish therein, you want to cast suspicion over a number of characters in your novel. You want to cast suspicion over the characters you have chosen as your suspects (three to six of them), and, in addition, you want to cast suspicion on other characters in the book. Let's call these other characters *outliers* — people who seem to be outside the scope of the main plot and the main suspicions, but are still possible of being the villains. In fact, whether or not you deliberately cast suspicion on an outlier, some readers will conclude that a certain outlier is the murderer.

When writing, feel free to cast suspicion over many of the characters in your book. Feel even freer to cast it often. Once just won't do. Readers may forget one incident, but they won't forget a buildup of incidents, one after the other.

When I wrote *Dirty Proof* I tried to cast suspicion on all of the main characters. But by the time I was writing *Sound Proof* I had learned enough to plan and control whom I wanted readers to suspect. Because there are two main solutions in *Sound Proof* — the solution of the murder and the solution of the instrument thefts — I made two separate charts of suspects. For the purposes of this book, I'll reproduce only one of these working charts: the chart of murder suspects.

In order to make my writing more effective (to cast suspicion where I wanted it cast), I listed which characters I definitely wanted the reader to suspect. These are under *Yes*. I also wanted a large group of *Maybe* characters: some readers would suspect these people, some wouldn't. And I wanted to be aware of which characters readers most likely would not suspect. These I labeled *Probably Not*.

Murder Suspects in the Reader's Mind

Yes	Maybe	Probably Not
Raven Hook	Nola Grayson	Suzanne Quering
Edric English	Cindy Ruffo	Sheriff Yale Davis
Vance Jurasek	Fonnie Sheffler	Bliss Beckins
Booker Hayes	Sheriff Yale Davis	Aja Freeman
Lafayette Wafer	Kim Oberfeld	Jeff Glover
Mary Ployd	Guy Dufour	Kofi Quay
		Tansy Thompson
		Cody Thompson

Who the reader suspects is mostly (but not entirely) under your control. Consider who you want the reader to suspect, and write accordingly. Consider who you don't want the reader to suspect, and write accordingly.

In *Dirty Proof*, in which the murderer is one of the main characters, I wanted the reader to suspect not only him, but several other characters, all at the same time. That is, I wanted the reader to be undecided about which of the main suspects committed the crime.

In *Sound Proof*, however, in which the murderer is a minor character, I did not want the reader to suspect this character. This meant I would have to plant clues that I wanted the reader to overlook — so that when the solution came, the reader would remember the clues and feel satisfied. More about this in the chapter on planting clues.

Motives for Murder

That you need to cast suspicion on many of your characters is a given in mystery writing. The main way you go about doing this is by providing the characters with one, two, or three of the following: Motive to commit the crime; Means to commit the crime; Opportunity to commit the crime. Of these, motive commands the highest reader interest. Readers know from personal experience that people have motives for doing certain things. Readers themselves have motives for doing certain things. Sometimes motives are good, sometimes bad. Sometimes relevant, sometimes not. But people enjoy examining and questioning motives, so it's **motive** that you will spend the most time developing for each of the characters you want the reader to suspect.

In this book I'll discuss motive, means, and opportunity in two different chapters. In this chapter I talk about how a writer attributes one or more of these to characters in order to have readers suspect these characters. In chapter fourteen I'll talk about how a writer works to *hide* the motive, means, or opportunity of the villain. On the one hand, you want readers to suspect . . . the wrong people. On the other hand, you want readers to not suspect . . . the villain.

Motives for murder are sometimes bizarre, but usually they boil down to money, power, love/hate, jealousy, revenge, or saving face (such as keeping a secret from getting out). In *Dirty Proof* the motive for murder is keeping a secret. In *Sound Proof* the motive for murder is revenge. I think that monetary gain and the gaining of power are more common motives for murder in real life, but I personally have found it difficult to plot a mystery in which the motive is financial gain, only because I think such a motive would *really* stand out and move the character to the head of the suspects line. But hundreds if not thousands of mystery writers have chosen to use financial gain as the motive for their villains and have done an excellent job of casting suspicion in such a way that the reader doesn't assume there's only one suspect. Often that involves withholding information about a particular financial gain until the end of the book. That is, the detective doesn't discover this fact until the end of the book. More about this in the chapter on motive, means, and opportunity.

I find motives of revenge and keeping a secret interesting to write about not only because they allow me to develop characters who are motivated by revenge or keeping a secret, but also because these motives are often hard to discover, so the detective has to do some real digging to find them.

If the villain is a major character in your novel, then bring out his or her possible motives early in the novel. Unless, as I said, you need to disguise something about about his or her financial gain. Even then, you will need to cast suspicion on the villain through other means, so that when the financial gain is revealed, the reader won't say, "Oh, that's unfair, I never would have suspected this person!" You *do* want the reader to suspect your villain a bit — but maybe not for the right reasons. That is, you might want the reader to suspect your villain because of *opportunity*, not motive. So the reader will know all along that Character X had the opportunity to commit the crime . . . but that alone proves nothing. It may be a reason for suspecting somebody, but it isn't proof. More about that in the chapter on solutions.

If your villain is a minor character, you may or may not want to cast suspicion on him. After all, one of the reasons for choosing a minor character as the villain is so that you can surprise the reader (in a good way). And so that you can pull off a "least likely suspect" story successfully. Just recently I read Antonio Hill's first police-detective novel, *The Summer of Dead Toys*, in which the villain was a minor character seemingly beyond suspicion. I found the solution satisfying, though, because the author had planted clues. (I had overlooked the hints, but they were there.)

Even though you might not want to cast suspicion on a minor character (as Hill most likely didn't want to in *The Summer of Dead Toys*, as I definitely didn't want to in *Sound Proof*), you will still need to plant clues about his or her motive, means, and opportunity throughout the book, so that when the detective solves the case, there is no confusion or cry of "Unfair!" on the part of the reader. Always play fair with the reader. Playing fair makes your job of blurring suspicions and hiding clues in plain sight much more difficult. But your work will result in much greater reader enjoyment.

In *Sound Proof* the motive for murder (revenge) is not *fully* revealed until chapter twenty-seven, the penultimate chapter. And even then, once the motive is revealed, it's not clear who the killer is. Nevertheless, hints at the motive are plentiful throughout the book, starting with the very first scene, in which Stubbs denies people what they want.

But until the very end of the novel, the reader doesn't know what the motive for murder was. And that's the way you as a writer want it, because that means you can cast suspicion on the motives of several characters. For example, I cast suspicion on Raven in such a way that readers will think she's jealous of Mary's success *and* that she wants revenge on Stubbs because he divorced her for a younger wife.

Means of Murder

Giving characters motives for the crime is the single best way of casting suspicion on them. But you also need to give them the **means** of committing the crime. Their having the means in turn casts suspicion on them. Think of means as method, manner, way, ability, or technique. If in your novel the victim is poisoned, then any character who has knowledge of poisons and/or access to them has the means or method with which to kill. They are thus suspect. And as I mentioned in an earlier chapter, always research everything that appears in your novel, *especially* the means of murder. (It seems that there are an awfully lot of mystery readers who know what does and does not work when it comes to murder.)

In *Dirty Proof*, once Frank eliminated other suspects, he realized that the murderer had to be somebody who had agility, strength, and speed of a certain kind. The means of committing the crime narrowed the field of suspects greatly toward the end of the story.

You can trick the reader into thinking a certain character does *not* have the means to commit the crime, but then reveal later in the book that she does. I think of Golden Age mysteries or movies in which Character X is always in a wheelchair and we're told she can't walk. But then it's revealed toward the end of the book that she *can* walk, and that she committed the murder. This type of "means" revelation has been done to death, so to speak, so if you use it, plant your clues very carefully, so that readers won't feel you unfairly withheld something from them.

If you choose a highly specialized method of murder, capable of being committed by only a few people, then you will need to take pains to either have several of your characters capable of this method of murder, or to have it appear that none (or all!) are capable of this method of murder.

In *Sound Proof* I chose to have Stubbs bludgeoned to death while sleeping. If Stubbs had been wide awake when the killer attacked with a hammer, it's possible that Stubbs could have overcome the killer. Or shouted out. Or inflicted some blows on the killer. So that, even if Stubbs were still murdered, investigators would make certain assumptions about the size and (probably) sex of the offender. One doesn't expect a woman to walk up to somebody and start bludgeoning them. But when the victim is initially asleep, anybody, large or small in stature, could creep up on them and strike a first deadly blow. In *Sound Proof* just about everybody had the *means* of killing Stubbs.

Throughout the novel I planted the suspicion that Frank's stolen hammer was the murder weapon. Thus any character associated with a hammer (Raven, Mary, Guy, Jeff Glover, Kim Oberfeld) might be suspected by readers.

Opportunity for Murder

Opportunity, like motive, is something you can give many, if not all, of the characters in your novel. That will increase reader suspicion. Or you can make it appear that only four of your five suspects had the opportunity to commit murder, but then near the end reveal that the fifth suspect also had an opportunity but hid it or lied about it, or somebody alibied him.

One of the things I as a reader enjoy when reading a mystery is trying to keep straight in my mind who had the opportunity to commit the crime and who didn't. I always figure that the murderer is one of those who had the opportunity. If a character did not have the opportunity to commit the crime, I tend to not count her as a suspect. Even though, as I stated in the previous paragraph, a writer may sometimes reveal near the end that what was assumed is incorrect. If this is done honestly, with some contradictions planted throughout the story, then I'm very happy to have been fooled.

In *Dirty Proof* only the characters who were present at the *Truth-Examiner* building late the night of the murder had the opportunity to commit the crime. That narrowed the field considerably. But in *Sound Proof* just about every character had the opportunity to commit the crime, and that's because it occurred around midnight, inside Stubbs' RV, in a place (the festival grounds) where musicians and vendors walk around day and night and nobody thinks a thing of it.

You can provide few or many characters in your novel with motive, with means, and with opportunity. Which of these you want to be the most important of the three is up to you. But as a writer, think about them in a logical way and make decisions about what you want to reveal and what you want to hide — all for the purpose of casting (or not) suspicion on certain of your characters.

Back-and-Forth vs. Linear

You can cast suspicion upon your characters in a back-and-forth manner or in a linear manner. You can organize your chapters in such a way that the reader changes who she suspects each time a different character is featured. You can have characters cast suspicion on one another, usually by what they reveal to the detective, willingly or grudgingly. Here's an example of what the back-and-forth manner might look like if you have five suspects. As you can see by the diagram, A casts suspicion on both C and E. B also casts suspicion on C, who casts it on D, who casts in on B, who casts it on A.

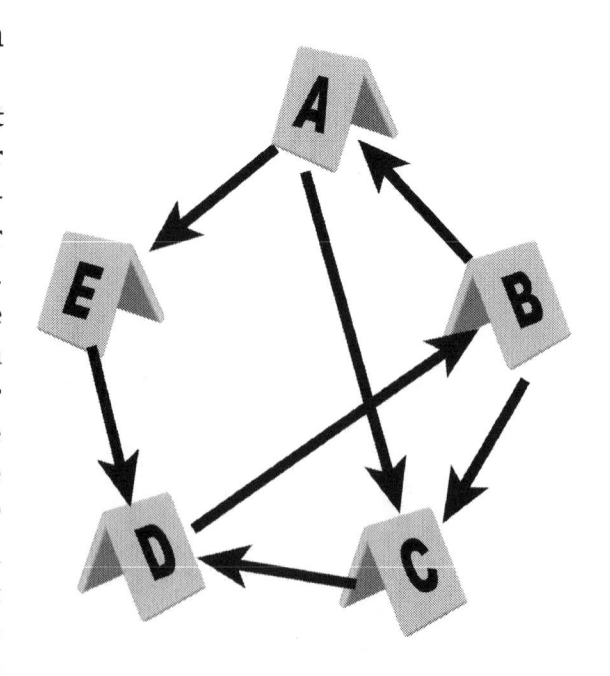

The back-and-forth method allows you (and your detective)

to go from one suspect to another. And then back, in no random pattern. Perhaps one suspect implicates another, or says something that leads the detective to an inference. This method has the advantage of moving the plot forward in perhaps unpredictable ways, and also of keeping the reader guessing.

If you cast suspicion on your characters in a linear manner, a chart might look something like this:

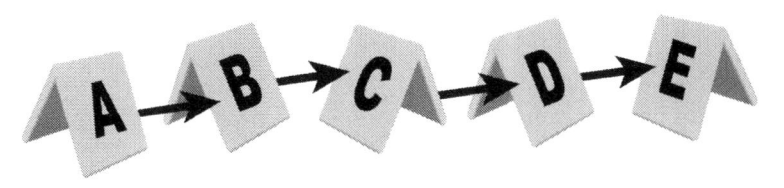

A → B → C → D → E

When you cast suspicion on your characters in a linear manner, with the detective pretty much exhausting one character and one set of clues before moving on to the next, you do *not* want your story to end with the final character being the villain. That is just too obvious, and your readers will probably pick up on this pattern by the time the detective is investigating the third character.

If you're using the linear method of casting suspicion, you want the villain to turn out to be one of the earlier suspects, so that the reader is pleasantly surprised. The chart might look like this:

A → B → C → D → E
     ↖_____╱

Readers and *Sound Proof* Suspects

In writing *Sound Proof* I used something like the linear method, and I plotted it in this manner:

Festival Day	Who I Want Reader to Suspect Most
End of Monday	Raven
End of Tuesday	Edric
End of Wednesday	Booker
End of Thursday	Lafayette
End of Friday	Vance

Whether readers suspected the characters in the order I wanted them to, or when I wanted them to, I don't know. But immediately after *Sound Proof* was published I sent out a survey asking readers to participate by emailing me who they suspected the murderer was by the time they reached the end of chapter fourteen, which is halfway through the novel.

Answers were all over the map. Some suspected Raven, but more suspected Mary. Many suspected Lafayette and Vance. A few suspected Guy Dufour. Three or four people suspected Opal Jackson, who is not even "in" the book. She is mentioned as having been Stubbs' first wife, but she doesn't appear other than by mention. Yet that didn't stop people from suspecting her at the halfway mark. Which, to be honest, I hoped a few people would do!

So you see that mystery readers are a highly suspecting bunch, and sometimes you have only to *mention* a character in order to have somebody suspect her. In any case, I took the results of this survey as evidence that I did my job well. I wanted to cast suspicion on at least five characters, and reader results show that I succeeded in doing that.

Planting Clues

The casting of suspicion is different from the planting of clues. The former is broader and more diffuse. Even when suspicion is cast over one character in particular, it hovers like a wide, dark cloud over his head — ominous, perhaps, but neither exact nor specific.

A clue, on the other hand, is specific and exact. It's a piece of evidence such as a scrap of clothing, a footprint, a bank statement, an overheard conversation, records of phone calls, or a blood smear.

A writer plants clues throughout a mystery for several reasons. First, the detective needs to uncover clues during her investigation. If not, the story will lie dead in the water and the reader will be disappointed. In literature, as in real life, we leave clues everywhere — our fingerprints, our DNA, scraps of paper, fibers from our clothes, photographic evidence that we were at a certain place at a certain time, and so on. A detective must have clues to find.

Second, and equally important to the first reason, is that mystery readers want to be able to pick up on clues themselves: to decide what is and is not a clue, and what it might mean. Planting clues is playing fair with the reader. Failing to plant clues is playing false with the reader.

Plant Many Clues

The mystery writer is always planting evidence, but not all evidence points to the same suspect. There may be twenty clues within one novel, but perhaps only three of them point to the villain. While the writer knows what's what, the reader will have a difficult but enjoyable time trying to figure out which evidence is important and who it points to. Plant many clues, and plant them on many of your suspects. The more clues you plant, the easier it will be to bury the two or three most important ones within the mass of clues.

As a writer you can make your clues obvious (blood smears, for example) or you can make them subtle (the dog that didn't bark in the nighttime). All of your clues can be obvious, or you can mix it up with some clues obvious, other clues subtle. Choices such as this often depend on the writer's outlook and style: what he or she enjoys in a good mystery. If all your clues are obvious ones, then something else needs to complicate the mystery, because obvious clues tend to be more easily resolved. If, for example, ballistics matches the fatal bullet to a gun owned by David, then it's likely that David is the killer. Unless you complicate that obvious clue with other factors . . . the gun was stolen a year ago . . . David was in Quebec at the time . . . the barrel of the gun was tampered with . . . and so on.

If, on the other hand, all of your clues are subtle ones, then both the detective and the reader need to be very observant to pick up on them. When you're planting a subtle clue, draw attention *away* from it by coming up with something immediately following it — a shout, a shot, an angry interjection, a fight, a joke. These will serve to draw reader attention away from the importance of the subtle clue.

The importance of some clues can be obvious from the moment they appear: a footprint in the mud, say. The importance of other clues (a car that wouldn't start) might not be understandable until that clue is linked with something else near the end of the book.

Not all of the clues should point to the villain. Some should point to innocent people. In *Sound Proof*, the cut fiddle strings wound around the neck of Stubbs' red fiddle point to Lafayette Wafer, who is innocent of murder. Having many clues will give your detective more information to sift through. Likewise, your readers will have a harder (and therefore more enjoyable) time determining which clues are relevant and which are not.

It's best to space out your clues within the story. Agatha Christie was a master of this: sometimes an event or conversation at the very beginning of the book, before the murder takes place, is key to the solution of the crime. Start early with your clues and keep them up throughout the book. But remember: only some of these clues will point to the solution. The others are red herrings (a red herring being a clue that is misleading).

Last of all, it might work best to plant most of your clues *after* you finish the first draft. By the time you reach the end of your first draft, you know how the detective solves the crime. Now you need to make certain that this is a solution the reader deems *fair*: the reader feels she could have reached the same conclusion if only she had realized the significance of the clues. This is best accomplished by reading your first draft and making notes about where you can plant a clue and what kind of clue it will be: a clue of misdirection? a clue that's important to the solution?

Then, having written these clue notes on your first draft, you can take a break of a month or so before you actually start the second draft. In your second draft you'll be concentrating on major questions such as character, plot, motivation, and pacing. (More about this in the chapter on rewriting.) In concentrating on these big questions, you might overlook the proper planting of clues throughout the book. That's why it's better, in my opinion, to make notes on the first draft as soon as you finish it.

Some Clues from *Sound Proof*

That said, here are some clues from *Sound Proof*. In each case I'm reproducing only one or two sentences and within them I'm boldfacing the clue. In each case the clue is something that helps Frank Dragovic put together the whole story and solve the mysteries. (Remember that there are three crimes: instrument theft; blackmail; and murder.)

Chapter 1
"Waydell Ames would have taught us," someone said.
"**Waydell's dead,**" Stubbs retorted.

. . .

"There you'd be, all lonesome and sad, just you and the dark and the rain. What would you be thinking? **I know you'd be wishing you could do things over.**

This would be something you'd wish you had done different." She paused. "But then it would be too late."
I stared at Mary, whose words carried an overtone of threat.

Chapter 2
Alongside her chair sat a beat-up old guitar case: black cardboard held together with duct tape. **Fonnie stared at the musicians as if memorizing them. Or maybe their instruments.**

. . .

"Just stack them here," he indicated. Glover looked to be in his fifties. **He walked slightly off kilter, favoring his left leg.**

. . .

I nodded. According to Mary, **all the royalties she earned from "Jealous Man" went into improving the farm as a festival site.**

. . .

A hammer lay on the dirt floor near the door. I didn't like tools lying on the floor. "Yours?" I asked as I handed it to Raven.

Chapter 3
I checked out the RVs and campers next, but they were harder to look into. **Fonnie Sheffler's grizzled Chesapeake camper was anchored next to Stubbs' Roadtrek,** and next to him stood Kim Oberfeld's Chevy truck with a Coleman folding trailer attached to its bed.

. . .

"He's always climbing," she said, turning to me. **"And stay away from the black walnut tree, you hear me, Cody?"**

I entered Mary's office, closing the door behind myself.

Mary was also on the phone. "That's right, Mary," she said. "You take care, now. Call me if you need me. Bye."

"That was Mary Ames," Mary explained. "**Waydell's sister.** She's feeling bad."

. . .

Stubbs made a desperate leap for the fiddle **just as Glover, who had been talking to another customer, turned with a scowl.**

Stubbs gasped like a fish out of water and staggered backward, clutching his chest.

. . .

Pushing his tea away, Lafayette fidgeted with the multiple parts of **his Leatherman — screwdriver, awl, wire cutter, pliers, saw, scissors.**

Chapter 4

I pulled a chair into the circle between Cody Thompson and Jeff Glover, who was apparently taking time off from selling bones, fiddles, mandolins, and knives. "Kim's watching my booth," he explained as if reading my mind. "Don't get much African drumming out in Wyoming."

I dropped my tool belt alongside the chair. As usual, sawdust and more important contents spilled out — an occupational hazard of carpenters. My father, who taught me carpentry, also taught me to look around for any dropped items before picking up my tool belt.

. . .

We were all still communing with our drums when the sound of a man howling in despair rolled across the fields and into the pole barn. **Before the others could even leave their seats, I was out of mine, racing out the door and up the hill.**

Chapter 5

"Nobody was around. **It's hot as blazes."**

So what was she doing on the top of an aluminum camper, getting toasted like a crostini, top and bottom?
"You didn't see anybody go into Vance's tent?"

• • •

When it didn't appear, I broadened my search to the area outside the chairs. **"Somebody took my hammer,"** I said.

"Mary has hammers," Kofi replied. "She will loan you one."

• • •

En route to the showers I stopped by the vendor area to ask Jeff Glover if he'd seen my hammer. He said he hadn't. **"I'd offer to loan you mine,"** he said, **"but Guy Dufour borrowed it this morning."**

• • •

I moved down the line of vendor tables to Kim Oberfeld's booth. **A straight-claw Klein was lying on top of a stack of song books. I picked it up. Not mine.** I returned it to its paperweight function. "Somebody took my hammer," I explained, "right after the drumming class. Have you seen anybody walking around with it?"

• • •

Back at the tent I cleaned off my black running shoes, **spread my wet clothes on the grass to dry,** and laid out the clothes I'd be working in tonight: an old "Good Guys Wear Black" Sox T-shirt and a pair of black jeans. Too hot for them now.

Burying and Deflecting

There are several things to notice about the clues listed above.

As I stated earlier, they're small — small pieces of factual information that in most cases are only part of an entire sentence.

Further, in most cases the value of the clues is deflected by something else that immediately follows. The clues are "buried" within information that at the time seems more important to the forward progression of the story. For example, the clue "Waydell's dead" seems to characterize Shelby Stubbs as callous and serves to further stun or anger the musicians clustered around him. Only later in the story (much later) is Waydell's death connected to the murder.

In the hammer clues I complicate matters in order to deflect attention away from Jeff Glover and onto others. I complicate by indicating that Raven has Mary's hammer, Kim Oberfeld has a hammer, and Guy Dufour borrowed Jeff's hammer. My intent was to make the borrowing of hammers confusing enough that readers wouldn't even try to keep track of it. But at the same time, I wanted readers to think that all the borrowing of hammers was a clue to something. In reality, the *borrowing* is a red herring, as it has nothing to do with the theft of Frank's hammer.

Further still, the clues are in every chapter, and they just keep on coming. I haven't counted the total number of clues in *Sound Proof,* but I'll bet they number at least fifty. Part of the reason for such a high number is that there are three crimes within the novel, each having its own clues. I'm not saying that mysteries need fifty clues!

In *Sound Proof* I wrote a mystery with many clues: in *Dirty Proof* I wrote one with few clues. It is perfectly possible to write a mystery with few clues. For example, you might want a story in which it appears there are no clues whatsoever, but, in reality, there are one or two clues that it takes your detective a while to figure out. On the other hand, you might want to write a mystery like *Murder on the Orient Express,* in which dozens and dozens of clues overwhelm the reader and point to just about everyone.

Planting clues is one of the most enjoyable parts of writing mysteries. Think them up and scatter them throughout your book.

14 Disguising of Motive, Means, and Opportunity

Although I discussed motive, means, and opportunity in an earlier chapter, what I talked about there was the writer's need to develop motive for various characters in the novel and to use motive, means, and opportunity to cast suspicion on the major characters in the novel. In this chapter I will talk about the necessity of disguising one or more of this trio, so that the reader doesn't immediately figure out who the villain is.

Motive First

Most readers are most interested in motive. That is, they're more interested in motive than they are in means or opportunity. They want to know what a character's motives are. They may speculate on a character's motives well before the author reveals these things. In our daily lives we often speculate on what a person's motives are: *Why did my boss say that to me? What's the government's real reason for the new gasoline tax? Why didn't Clarissa invite me to her party?*

Motive is what readers find fascinating . . . and necessary. When a prosecutor tries a case, she ascribes a probable motive to the person on trial — whether or not that motive is real, whether or not it led to theft, murder, blackmail, or whatever. Juries need to hear motive. As do readers of mysteries.

While crimes are solved by a detective considering who has the motive, who has the means, and who has the opportunity, the fact is that without motive, means and opportunity are dead in the water. Just because a character had the opportunity to murder doesn't mean she did. Just because a character had the means to murder, doesn't mean she did. But if she had a motive, a means, and an opportunity, then she may very well be the murderer.

It's good to give possible motives for the crime to several of your characters. At the same time it's important for you as a writer to hide or disguise the actual motive of the villain — so that your detective has to work hard to discover it, and so that your reader has to work hard, too. Readers love working to solve a mystery, and when their work leads them to the correct solution, they feel great satisfaction with the book. Conversely, they feel less satisfaction if they know the solution within the first 50-100 pages.

Economic gain is a prevalent motive, but also one that's difficult to disguise. If the villain's motive is economic gain, disguise this motive or gain as well as you can. Laurie King does a masterful job of disguising the economic gain in *Justice Hall*. As a result, she of course does a masterful job of disguising who had the motive for this gain. Although disguising economic gain is difficult to do well, especially in today's computer age, where all kinds of public records are accessible, it can be used and hidden.

In disguising economic motive you might want to consider a reverse solution, or what I call working backward. That is, on the surface things may look as if Carlton has an economic motive to murder his aunt, because he stands to inherit her fortune. But perhaps somebody knows that Carlton's aunt was looking into selling her estate to developers, who would turn it into a shopping mall, whereas the same somebody knows that Carlton would want to keep the estate intact. This somebody murders Carlton's aunt before she can sell the estate. But then suspicion falls on Carlton. The murderer (who wants Carlton to inherit) doesn't want that, so the murderer works hard to hinder the detective's investigation, maybe even going so far as to give Carlton a false alibi for the time of the murder. What I mean by "working against expectations" is that the motive is not economic gain, but rather the prevention of somebody else's economic gain (the aunt's).

Disguising the motives of rivalry, revenge, and protecting a secret are slightly easier than disguising economic gain. Making the motive the protection of a secret doubles the amount of work your detective hero will do. First she has to uncover that there *is* a secret, then she must discover what the secret is, and then she must determine how many people are affected by the secret, and then which of them had the most to fear or the most to lose if the secret were exposed.

Motives in *Sound Proof*

In *Sound Proof* I used economic gain as the motive for the thief, rivalry as the motive for the blackmailer, and revenge as the motive for the murderer.

The instrument theft motive was pretty straightforward, but I disguised the thief in several different ways:

> (1) The thief is poor and also envious and wants to make easy money, but many of the musicians at Mary's festival are poor, so the thief doesn't stand out in this respect.
> (2) By sheer luck (my plotting), the thief sold one of the stolen instruments to Lafayette, who bartered it to Booker, who then sold it to Bliss. So on the surface suspicion falls heavily on Booker. This all serves to distract the reader from Fonnie, the real thief.
> (3) I created Vance, a character who seems to covet instruments of all kinds, and I placed him in charge of the hurdy-gurdy that, under his "watch," was stolen. I also placed his tent very close to Fonnie's camper.

The blackmail motive (rivalry) was easier to disguise for the simple reason that Mary refuses to say why she's being blackmailed, and it takes Frank Dragovic more than half of the book to determine what the blackmail was about. And, because throughout the book Mary obviously wants her expensive guitar to be stolen, readers may assume, as Frank at first does, that there's a connection between the blackmail notes and the instrument thefts.

Similarly the revenge motive was easier for me to disguise than was the economic motive, partly because the revenge is for an act that occurred thirty-some years earlier. Waydell Ames, one of the people involved in the act, dies just a few weeks before Midwest Music Madness begins. Stubbs, another of the people involved in the act, is murdered. And Mary is too ashamed to bring up the incident, no matter how many times and from how many directions Frank tries to get the information from her.

With the revenge motive, my problem was not how to disguise the motive, but rather how to bring it out! I did that partly through Lafayette, who knew both Stubbs and Mary when they were all young. Lafayette makes allusions to the past that Frank begins to piece together. I did it partly through Frank's strong belief that somebody is trying to murder Mary. And partly through Mary's extreme reaction when she hears the song "Oh, the Wind and the Rain." Finally, I also alluded to the past through Stubbs' will, in which he leaves everything "to my first and only wife."

I've discussed the primary motives, but they aren't the only ones, and maybe in your planned novel you have a different, unusual motive for the crime. Go for it, I say. One of my favorite mysteries is *A Place of Execution*, by Val McDermid. Once you read it, you will never forget the motive for that particular murder.

Opportunity

Many times mystery writers will give the villain a strong motive that is discovered fairly early in the story, but then give the villain no seeming opportunity to have committed the crime. This is as should be. Opportunity, like means, is not intrinsically interesting in and of itself. Opportunity becomes interesting only when it appears that the main suspect(s) could not have committed the crime. Then the detective needs to prove that an alibi is false: prove that, in fact, the murderer could indeed have been present at the time of the murder. Sometimes writers go to great lengths to hide and/or prove opportunity. In Dorothy Sayers' *Five Red Herrings* time tables play a predominant role in helping to prove opportunity.

The opposite of making it appear that the villain had no opportunity to commit the crime is to give each of the main suspects the opportunity to commit the crime. This is a common solution to the question of who had the opportunity — if every suspect had the opportunity, then opportunity is a "wash." It doesn't help determine who committed the crime.

Means

It's been said that the gun is the "great equalizer" in that just about anybody can pull a trigger and thus commit murder. This is one of the reasons why, in modern mysteries in which a gun is the murder weapon, the *means* (method) of murder is often less critical to the solution of the crime than it is in a mystery set in the past.

Take, for example, the Brother Cadfael novels by Ellis Peters. In these novels, set in England during the twelfth century, murder is sometimes by poison, sometimes by sword, by knife, by cudgel. Because it takes great skill to wield a sword, and because not everybody had access to knives, nor the strength to wield a cudgel, the *means* of murder often help Cadfael narrow down the suspects. And in novels such as Nero Wolfe's *Fer-de-Lance* and Dorothy Sayers' *Strong Poison*, suspicion falls on those who had knowledge of and access to certain poisons. If your mystery features an arcane method of murder, then be certain to disguise which of the characters possesses the knowledge and skill of obtaining and/or using this method. You can disguise this by having it seem that nobody has this knowledge, or you can disguise it by indicating that two or three of the suspects have this knowledge.

In a modern mystery the question of the means of murder can center not on the gun itself (if it is a gun), but on who had the means of obtaining a gun, or even that particular gun. In *Sound Proof* the murder weapon is a hammer, but not much strength or skill is needed to strike a sleeping man on the head with a hammer, and then to continue striking until the victim is dead. So while a hammer seems to be a man's weapon, I made certain that throughout the novel hammers were associated with women, too.

In summary, you as a writer decide whether you will emphasize motive, means, or opportunity . . . or two of the trio, or all three. You also decide how to disguise the relationship between the villain and this trio. In making these decisions, you are also deciding how your detective will unravel the crime: by uncovering motive, by revealing opportunity, or by discovering means. As I mentioned in the chapter on planting clues, make certain to disguise the solution by burying the clues in small pieces throughout the book. Or by raining down so many clues that the reader doesn't know which are relevant and which aren't.

If you're the kind of writer who proceeds without a clear plan or an outline, then chances are you will think up motives, means, and opportunity well into the book. If so, then during your first rewrite you may need to break up your original clues into smaller chunks. If you find your clues appearing in large clumps, separate them and scatter them throughout the book, making them less easy to detect. Motive, means, and opportunity: you want them present throughout the novel, though in hard-to-detect form.

Think of the planting of clues (previous chapter) and the disguising of motive, means, and opportunity as watering a garden with a sprinkling can rather than with a power hose — little drops of water will soak into the soil and saturate it evenly, allowing your plot to grow and your readers to feel satisfied. A power hose will leave an obvious ditch-like streak, disguising nothing — and perhaps washing away the plot that you really want to develop.

Timelines

Anyone who has had a history class has undoubtedly seen a timeline, which is a graphic representation of time depicted on a line with divisions marked off proportionately. Timelines can represent entire epochs, in which the divisions may be in millions of years; they can represent centuries, in which the divisions may be in 100-year increments; or they can represent years, months, weeks, days, or even hours or seconds.

Most mysteries don't include timelines: there's no need for the writer to ramp up the tension by including a ticking clock or a progressing timeline. Mystery and thriller writers do sometimes include datelines or hours or minutes at the beginning of chapters in order to increase the tension: *how many days are left before the killer strikes again? how many seconds left to defuse the bomb?* And so on.

Invisible Timelines

The timelines I've mentioned above are timelines that readers see. But there are also timelines that readers don't see, and these are the timelines a writer may make for herself so that she can judge the pacing, suspense, or tension in her novel. I usually write without constructing a timeline, but for *Sound Proof* I found that I needed one in order to help me plot the story better. What I constructed might better be called a time chart than a timeline, but whatever it's called, it serves the purpose of showing which events occurred during a particular period.

There are several reasons why I felt I needed to construct a timeline for *Sound Proof*. First, the story takes place over a five-day festival, Monday through Friday. Second, there are three separate crimes in the novel. Third, there are many characters.

To control all the things I've talked about in previous chapters (plot, characters, plenty of clues, suspicion, and so on), to make certain that I used a sprinkling can rather than a power hose to develop the story, I created a timeline which covered the period from Monday through Friday. Each division was one full day. Each division could have been part of a day, such as morning, afternoon, and evening, but I didn't want to feel constrained in that manner. On the timeline, I listed the main events that occurred on that day.

At first glance you might think: this is an outline, not a timeline. But that isn't so. Outlines are far more detailed. Further, the outline would be a chapter-by-chapter outline, hence it would have twenty-eight divisions, not five. Also, outlines are generally long, from two to twenty pages. It's impossible to "glance" at a 28-chapter outline and instantly grasp whether there's enough going on in each day. In addition, my chapter outline isn't divided into

Monday	Tuesday	Wednesday	Thursday	Friday
Stubbs offends all	Sheriff grills Frank	Stubbs changed his will	Blackmailer caught	Lafayette honors Mary
Mary's guitar on stoop	Lafayette hated Stubbs	Sheriff grills Raven	Raven took hammer	Classes prepare tunes
Stubbs faints	Frank questions Guy	Frank's clothes bloody	Shelby intended to leave	Sheriff suspects Edric
Frank repairs pigpen	Stubbs divorced Raven	Sheriff suspects Frank	Sheriff questions Frank	Frank suspects Sheriff
Edric's shoes stolen	Sheriff takes Edric in	Sheriff suspects Mary	Nola represents Frank	Frank finds guitar
Frank takes drumming	Nola talks about Stubbs	Frank finds fiddle	Nola's yard damaged	Thief is nabbed
Frank's hammer gone	Fonnie worships trees	Severe storm coming	Fonnie in town	Mary gives Bliss money
Stubbs murdered	First blackmail note	Edric talks to Frank	Frank takes drumming	Frank hears Mary's story
Stubbs' fiddle missing	Second blackmail note	Lafayette missing	Mary's guitar stolen	Bram was a victim
		Frank saves Lafayette	Vance reveals threat	Bram one of three men
		Lafayette confesses	Frank grills Mary	Glover, Jurasek, Davis
		Mary hysterical	Mary's plan fails	Bram is the killer
		Tree crashes		Frank guards Mary
				Mary leaves safety
				Glover grabs Mary
				Frank saves Mary

days. Rather, each day's story is told in either five or six chapters.

As you can see on the accompanying timeline for *Sound Proof*, this single sheet of paper allowed me to see the day's events at a glance. And when I glanced, I sensed that there wasn't enough rising action in my novel. Rising action is the subject of the next chapter, where I'll define the term and show you what changes I made to my timeline in order to increase rising action.

Timelines aren't necessary for every book, but I felt I needed one for a book based on time. Making this timeline, then analyzing it, helped me write a better story. If your novel is set over the course of a specific, finite period of time (one day, two days, a week), consider creating a timeline for yourself so that you can see the story's strengths and weak spots and act accordingly.

16 Rising Action and Pace

To hold a reader's interest and to both depict and resolve conflict, each novel requires rising action. The action need not be huge on a world scale, but the action is important to the character's development and the direction of the novel. The purpose of the rising action is to increase the stakes, thereby increasing tension and thereby increasing reader investment and interest.

For a visual explanation of rising action, many writing teachers and writing books show Freytag's pyramid. You can easily find many different examples of this plot pyramid on line. And there you'll notice that the rising action is depicted as a slanted line starting near the beginning of the novel and moving toward the northeast at a steep angle. In short, the action is going uphill, or rising.

Probably an easier way to visual rising action is to think of a staircase. At the very bottom (the ground floor) lies the beginning of your novel. From the beginning until perhaps the last two or three chapters, all the action must rise: step by step, the conflict must increase.

In the first chapter of my baseball novel, *She's on First*, the general question posed is, *Will a woman ever be signed to play major league baseball?* The more individual question (the one readers will be invested in) is, *Will Linda Sunshine play major league baseball?* In the first chapter the reader doesn't know, until the very end of the chapter, whether the major league scout will write a positive report on Linda and give it to the team owner. So the ground floor question is, *Will Linda Sunshine play?* and the first step of rising action is, *Will the scout recommend her?*

The second step of rising action is, *Will the owner sign her?*

The third step of rising action is, *Will the minor league manager play her?*

The fourth step is, *Will her teammates accept her?*

And so on and so on, each step increasing in tension, moving the story toward its climax and resolution.

Increase the Stakes

Just as in mainstream fiction, so in mysteries the stakes need to increase, the action needs to rise, the detective needs to move closer to the solution of the crime. In novel writing the great danger is the middle of the book — and in fiction the "middle" is considered to be everything except the first two chapters and the last two or three chapters. That's a huge middle! If your novel is thirty chapters long, then twenty-five of those chapters are the "middle" of your book.

It's important to know this because novels tend to bog down in the middle. Partly that's because the writer has so much to do — develop characters, write good narrative, create scenes, write dialogue, cast suspicion, plant clues, and so on — that she may proceed in good faith doing all of these things, but forget about rising action. As a result, the first draft (or second or third or fourth if this problem isn't corrected) drags. It reads slow. There are dead spots. Lulls. Long periods of sameness. That's because the writer hasn't been paying attention to the necessity of rising action.

Rising action need not occur in every single chapter of your novel: that could prove tedious to the reader. But there needs to be rising action at the rate of perhaps every second or third chapter.

Increase the stakes for your hero. Do this by whatever means seem appropriate for your story. In a mystery, one of the common ways of increasing the tension and stakes is to have a second murder take place, perhaps in the first third or first half of the book. Or a third murder.

Another way is to blindside the detective with some previously unknown information. Or a previously unknown person appears on the scene with vital information. Or somebody confesses but the detective doesn't believe that person committed the crime. Or persons unknown threaten or assault the detective. I'm sure you've encountered each of these examples many times in your reading. They're used over and over again because they work.

Your job is to make them seem believable within the context of your novel. And to put a fresh spin on them.

Amended Timeline

In the previous chapter I said that making a timeline and analyzing it helped me write a better novel. Here is the amended timeline, with the changes in boldfaced type.

Monday	Tuesday	Wednesday	Thursday	Friday
Stubbs offends all	Sheriff grills Frank	Stubbs changed his will	Blackmailer caught	Lafayette honors Mary
	Earlier death at MMM		**Hurdy-gurdy found**	**Booker's guitar stolen**
Mary's guitar on stoop	Lafayette hated Stubbs	Sheriff grills Raven	Raven took hammer	Classes prepare tunes
Stubbs faints	Frank questions Guy	Frank's clothes bloody	Shelby intended to leave	Sheriff suspects Edric
Frank repairs pigpen	Stubbs divorced Raven	Sheriff suspects Frank	Sheriff questions Frank	Frank suspects Sheriff
Edric's shoes stolen	Sheriff takes Edric in	Sheriff suspects Mary	Nola represents Frank	
Frank takes drumming	Nola talks about Stubbs	Frank finds fiddle	Nola's yard damaged	Thief is nabbed
Hurdy-gurdy stolen	**Cody finds Guy's tuner**	**Stolen instrument from previous festival found**	**Mary pushed, survives**	**Frank finds guitars**
Frank's hammer gone	Fonnie worships trees	Severe storm coming	Fonnie in town	Mary gives Bliss money
Stubbs murdered	First blackmail note	Edric talks to Frank	Frank takes drumming	Frank hears Mary's story
			Sealed letter to Nola	Bram was a victim
Stubbs' fiddle missing	Second blackmail note	Lafayette missing	Mary's guitar stolen	Bram one of three men
		Frank saves Lafayette	Vance reveals threat	Glover, Jurasek, Davis
		Lafayette confesses	Frank grills Mary	Bram is the killer
		Mary hysterical	Mary's plan fails	Frank guards Mary
		Tree crashes		Mary leaves safety
				Glover grabs Mary
				Frank saves Mary

You may recall that I said *Sound Proof* was not only organized over a period of five days, but that I depicted each day's events in five or six chapters. To be exact, here's how the events occur:

Monday — Chapters 1 - 6
Tuesday — Chapters 7 - 12
Wednesday — Chapters 13 - 18
Thursday — Chapters 19 - 23
Friday — Chapters 24 - 28

Originally the stakes for Frank Dragovic are that he must solve the instrument theft case by the end of the week. He spends the first day of the Midwest Music Madness festival studying the five main suspects, examining the location of their tents or campers, studying their habits, and examining the festival grounds for possible places one could temporarily stash a stolen instrument.

When I looked at my original timeline, I noticed that the only rising action came at the end of the sixth chapter, when Stubbs is murdered. That's one step upward in six chapters, which isn't enough. I sensed that the first day needed at least one more step of rising action. The way I solved this problem was to have Guy's hurdy-gurdy stolen in chapter four. This is an example of rising action. During Mary's previous festivals, the instrument thefts occurred on Friday. By creating an instrument theft on Monday, Frank's first day on the job, I up the ante for Frank and also for Mary Ployd, who fears people will stop coming to her festival.

Tuesday originally contained three occurrences of rising action: the sheriff questioning and suspecting Frank; Mary receiving a blackmail note; and Mary receiving a second blackmail note. All three of these up the stakes for Frank: but just as with the Monday timeline, I felt that something more was needed to increase reader interest. Earlier I mentioned that many mystery writers create a second murder as a means of rising action. While I have nothing against these second murders in principal, as a reader I've encountered too many of them, to the point where they don't *feel* as if they have raised the stakes. They feel expected, not unexpected. (Not in all cases, but in many.)

So, I didn't want to have a second murder.

But that didn't mean I couldn't have a second *death*.

An unexplained death.

A death that Mary, Frank's employer, has failed to mention.

And so I created a second death, one that occurred earlier than the start of the novel. And although I already had blackmail in the plot, I now tied the blackmail to the earlier death.

And, because I had inserted the hurdy-gurdy theft on Monday, I now continued that thread by having ten-year-old Cody Thompson find the tuner that Guy kept with his hurdy-gurdy. Cody finds it very near Lafayette's tent. This is an example of rising action, increasing the possibility that Lafayette stole the hurdy-gurdy.

When I looked at my original timeline for Wednesday, I felt it was full of rising action, culminating in the storm scene of chapter eighteen. However, all the rising action is in regard to the murder of Shelby Stubbs, none of it in regard to the stolen instruments. (Stubbs' missing fiddle is part of the murder scene, not necessarily part of the thefts.) So I thought it could only help intensify things if there were something more about instrument theft. But what?

That was when I came up with something out of the blue — why not have one of the instruments stolen in a previous year reappear in the hands of a musician? And then why not have the original owner, from whom the instrument was stolen, recognize her instrument and demand its return? I liked this idea a lot, so I went with it. The communal eating room scene in which this discovery takes place definitely increases the stakes, implicating Booker, and also driving home the point that although murder takes priority over theft (in any crime-solving hierarchy), Frank was hired to solve the thefts, and he is on the job.

One of the highlights (rising action) of the Thursday chapters is that the blackmailer is caught in the act — but also that she reveals what she knows about the murder and the murder weapon. Another example of rising action is that Mary's guitar, which she has been leaving on the porch throughout the festival, is stolen. The next piece of rising action is that Mary's plans to catch the thief fail in a big way. So now Frank has to find Mary's stolen guitar as well as the hurdy-gurdy. (He has already found Stubbs' fiddle.)

Several steps of rising action were part of the original Thursday timeline, but because the book was approaching the solution and end, I wanted even more rising action — the closer the book draws to its climax, the more steps of rising action are necessary. Or, if not more stairs, then more intense (steeper) stairs. While adding many rising steps at the beginning of the book might be confusing to readers (who sometimes need several chapters to absorb what's happening) adding them closer to the ending may be illuminating. And tense.

I chose to have Frank discover the stolen hurdy-gurdy on Thursday morning. This isn't exactly rising action, it's more "falling action" in that he is, if not solving the thefts, at least retrieving the stolen instruments. This step allowed me to close off the entire hurdy-gurdy theft and concentrate on the theft of Mary's guitar which, although it occurs much later in the book than the hurdy-gurdy theft, seems so much more personal on the part of the thief.

But I still wanted *more,* and actually began toying with the idea of a second murder. I rejected that and instead created an *attempt* on Mary Ployd's life. This is an example of rising action: if Frank doesn't determine who murdered Stubbs, Mary may end up dead.

I put in Mary's sealed letter to Nola (her attorney) as a small rising action step in that Mary's writing such a letter (to be opened only in the event of her death) indicates to both Frank and Nola that Mary Ployd knows something about the murder of Shelby Stubbs. But refuses to tell what it is.

With the Friday section I felt that the rising action of the last three chapters would meet reader expectations. But I thought that perhaps the first couple of short chapters on Friday could use a boost. So I added one more theft, that of Booker's guitar. This increases the stakes for Frank because things look worse than ever. Before he was hired, the thief stole one instrument per old time week. Once Frank is on the job, the thief steals *three* instruments in one week. This step makes it more important than ever for Frank to catch the thief.

Pace

Rising action is, as I said at the beginning of this chapter, a series of steps/incidents, each of which raises the stakes for the hero and/or raises the investment and tension for the reader.

Pace and pacing are something different. They aren't related to raising the stakes, necessarily, but are more related to the speed (pace) at which the novel proceeds and the reader experiences the story.

Most writing books which discuss pace and pacing talk about them interchangeably, as if they are the same thing. But I prefer to distinguish between pace and pacing so that you as a writer, no matter the pace of your novel, can still improve it with good pacing.

I think of pace as related to both personal temperament and world outlook. Because each of us is unique, with our own beliefs and interpretation of life, each of us will tell our stories at our own pace. On the day I'm writing this chapter, I'm reading Leonardo Padura's novel, *The Man Who Loved Dogs*. The book covers continents, spans decades, and contains many minor characters. The sentences are long, with many clauses, and as a result they take a while to read and comprehend. The pace of this novel reflects who Padura is, how he thinks, what he believes, and the story he wants to tell.

To understand pace in relationship to a mystery novel, think of one of P.D. James' Adam Dalgliesh mysteries: the pace of her books is slower than the pace of, say, a Rex Stout Nero Wolfe novel. Stout tells his stories in an economical manner. They don't span continents or decades. They have few subplots. And they're written in a more straightforward style than are James' books.

As I said, the pace of a novel reflects the author's outlook. A slower pace is not bad, a quicker pace is not good. Nor vice versa. It is what it is. You, as a reader, can gravitate toward one type of novel over another as a matter of reading preference . . . probably reflecting your disposition and world outlook. But as a writer you need not, for the most part, worry about the pace of your book, because your sentence structure and manner of proceeding with a story reflect who you are and how you see the world. Pace is inherent in each writer's style. (For an excellent analysis of how sentence structure reflects attitude, see Stanley Fish's *How to Write a Sentence: and How to Read One.*)

I say that you need not worry "for the most part" because it's possible you may want to write a Robert Parker Spenser-type novel but find that your sentences average 50 words each, there's almost no dialogue, and the manuscript is 600 pages long. Based on this evidence, I would say that your pace is not at all suited to a Spenser-type novel. Reconsider and try to emulate another mystery writer, one whose pace of story telling is more in keeping with yours.

Pacing

Pace relates to you (who you are, your world view). Pacing, on the other hand, relates to how the reader experiences the story. Many literary agents and editors say that the most frequent reason they return manuscripts is that the pacing isn't good.

What, then, is pacing?

It is, first and foremost, *a relationship between different parts of the story.* Between dialogue and narrative, for example. Between exposition and rising action. Between scene and summary. And between a lot of other aspects of story.

In a novel with good pacing the reader will never become tired or bored from reading long passages of description — because the writer will understand that most readers *do* become bored by reading long passes of description, and she will correct the pacing of her story to alternate any long descriptive passages with those containing conflict and dialogue.

Similarly, the writer needs to understand that, yes, people *do* become bored with chapter after chapter of nonstop action and cliff-hanger endings, and he will correct the pacing of his story to break up the monotony of action with narrative such as introspection on the part of the detective hero.

In writing, *pacing is the mixture of story-telling elements to produce a work that holds reader interest.* If you read mysteries by the hundreds or thousands, you will probably subconsciously pick up good pacing when you encounter it: you will know that there's something about that author's writing that you like (something in addition to the characters and the plot). You might not recognize that it's the pacing which keeps you interested, moving you and the plot forward with just the right amount of variation between scene and summary.

If you've been told that the pacing of your manuscript needs improvement, you can study a novel you admire and mark off the pacing in several consecutive chapters, writing NAR for Narrative, SC for Scene, and DI for Dialogue. Then, take an equal number of chapters or pages from your manuscript and mark them off using the same abbreviations. If you notice that your narrative goes on five times as long as the admired author's, and your scenes are one-third the length of the admired author's, you will begin to see how to improve the pacing of your novel.

I remember being a student in a fiction writing class at which each of us read the first chapter of our novels to the other students. After one student read, the teacher asked, "Could you please use a yellow marker to highlight the dialogue in your first chapter." The student had nothing to highlight: there was no dialogue in her first chapter. To her credit the student saw immediately that this was a problem in pacing, and the following week she rewrote the entire first chapter with better pacing — something that would keep readers interested.

There is no golden rule for good pacing, no advice that says something like, *3 paragraphs of narrative, 10 paragraphs scene, 2 paragraphs dialogue. Repeat to end of novel.* Good pacing is something you develop by writing and rewriting, and, most of all, by reading.

Scene and Summary in *Sound Proof*

Here are almost three pages from chapter eleven of *Sound Proof*. The first part is summary. The boldfaced part is scene.

> After lunch I went off to drum. Not going would offend Kofi, I rationalized. Not going would single me out as strange in a gathering where everybody played music. Admit the truth: I was here because I couldn't resist the drums.
>
> I caressed the goatskin drum head, savoring its

gritty texture. All of us stroked our drums in one way or another, practicing the patterns. I tried a few of the deep, satisfying booms. *Left right left right.* The volume filled my chest, the reverberations thrummed through my veins. Fingers flattened, I slapped the skin just past the outer edge, producing a higher pitched sound that wakened my brain.

Attuned to life, and in this case death, Kofi taught us a pattern played during Ewe funerals. Only part of the pattern, he explained: the whole pattern was very long and complex. The mourning seemed appropriate, the pattern healing. We had been drumming for maybe fifteen minutes when I noticed Bliss. Like a barefoot waif she stood in the doorway of the pole barn, one foot curled over the toes of the other. Kofi signaled *Stop* on the drum. We all stopped except Lafayette, who did so only when he realized nobody else was playing.

"Come in." Kofi motioned to Bliss. "We are playing a song of mourning. You will feel better. Come."

Bliss hesitated, then selected a drum and sat near Cody. The drumming resumed.

Yesterday I'd left the class feeling invigorated. Today it took prime energy to drag my ass out of the pole barn and up toward the main complex. I was tired and bad-tempered. My head hurt, I could barely keep my eyes open. I sniffed under my armpits. I stank. At the pigpen I stopped, leaned over the rail, and rested. I squinted up at the sun. If I tried to nap, I'd probably steam to death in the tent.

Suzanne was standing outside the kitchen, talking to Aja Freeman. After a couple of minutes, she left Aja and marched my way, practicing her bones, a pair in each hand. *One-TWO-three-FOUR, one-TWO-three-FOUR.*

"What's wrong?" she asked, imitating my posture by leaning on the rail. She held the bones in front of her, clicking them softly.

"What makes you think something's wrong?"

"Easy. You're hanging with the pig instead of with me."

I didn't reply.

"What's with all these cupolas?" she frowned, studying the one on the pig shed.

"Ventilation."

"Over-decoration, if you ask me. I'm glad the barn doesn't have one." She did something quick with the bones, a series of fast clicks.

"What's that you're doing?"

"Triplets." She smiled in satisfaction. "Not bad,

huh?"

"Yeah, I guess Best Bones West of the Mississippi would approve."

The triplets stopped a moment, then started up again. "What's wrong with you?" she asked.

"Did you know that Raven had been married to Shelby Stubbs?"

She snapped the bones loud enough to register three counties away. "I don't like it when you talk to me in that tone, Frank."

"What tone?"

"As if I'm holding out on you, as if I'm a suspect you're trying to extract information from!" She scowled at me.

"I need that kind of information to do the job I was hired to do."

Silence.

"Did you know?" I persisted.

"No!" she snapped, "I didn't know. I don't know these people like you think I do. Mary's the only one I know. What do I *care* who's married to who — you know how I feel about marriage anyway."

Right. Suzanne didn't believe in marriage, only in living together.

Except that she still wasn't living with me.

"You need a shower." She walked away, her body stiff.

"No, I don't," I retorted out of pure orneriness.

She turned and threw a bone at me. I caught it in my right hand. She threw another, I caught it in my left, barely. I thought she was going to throw the last two bones, but she turned and marched toward the farmhouse.

I looked at the bones in my hands: gray corners and sky-blue streaks winked back at me.

In *Sound Proof* this excerpt comes to twenty-two lines of summary and thirty-seven lines of scene. I start this particular chapter with summary but move into scene quickly. The scene isn't large, but *is* a scene: it takes place in real time, contains conflict, contains dialogue. So there is variety in the opening of chapter eleven: some narrative, some scene.

I'm not saying that I regularly write twenty-two lines of summary followed by thirty-even lines of scene. What I do is *alternate* scene and summary, pacing the book in a way that feels good to me: that is, it feels to me that this is the way my private eye would experience and report the story. And it feels to me that this is the way a reader would enjoy the telling of the story.

Everything works together to create a novel with good pacing — a story that will keep the reader engrossed through a combination of action and thought, scene and summary, dialogue and narrative.

Expositions and Beginnings

Exposition is information about events that happened before the beginning of the story, or information (technical information, for example) that the writer needs to impart in order for readers to understand the story. But the information itself is not part of the story: it is only part of events that occurred *before the story started* or *information the reader needs.*

All writers must learn how to handle exposition so that it reads naturally, doesn't interrupt the story, and doesn't clog up the narrative or dialogue of the story.

Here's an example of what I mean. In order to understand the beginning chapter of *Sound Proof,* the reader needs to be informed of the following:

> that Frank Dragovic is a private eye
> that he has been hired by Mary Ployd to find an instrument thief
> that Mary runs a summer music festival in Iroquois County, Illinois
> that the festival is named Midwest Music Madness
> that the instrument thief has stolen stringed instruments two years in a row
> that these thefts occurred during Old-time Music Week
> that Frank wants Suzanne Quering to move in with him
> that Mary Ployd used to be Suzanne's baby sitter years ago
> that Suzanne asked Frank to help Mary with the instrument thefts
> that Shelby Stubbs is teaching as a replacement for Waydell Ames
> that Frank is working undercover, posing as a carpenter

There are many ways a writer can handle this information. It could all appear somewhere in the first page of the book, as follows:

> It was because of Suzanne Quering that I was hired by Mary Ployd, organizer of Midwest Music Madness, to figure out who was stealing instruments during Old-time Week. That's what I do: figure out who's stealing things. Or blackmailing. Or killing. Usually, though, I don't encounter all of these in one case. This time I did.
>
> I wanted Suzanne to move in with me, but so far she was hesitating. So I thought I'd boost my chances by helping out her friend, Mary Ployd, when Suzanne asked me to. Mary had been Suzanne's babysitter twenty-some years ago. Now the three of us were on Mary's farm in downstate Iroquois County, in July, where the upper-nineties temperatures threatened to pop all the field corn at once. We weren't alone: another two hundred people were camping out on the farm, each of them taking one or more old-time music classes.
>
> Not all two hundred were potential thieves. Mary had that number narrowed down to five people — five people who had been at previous Madness festivals each time an instrument was stolen.
>
> Now I stood on the porch, pretending to be the festival carpenter, watching Shelby Stubbs interact with the musicians. Stubbs had been hired as a replacement for Waydell Ames, who died three weeks earlier.

In the example above, all the exposition comes at the beginning. This means that the actual story doesn't start until after the exposition is over. The exposition, remember, is *not* the story: it's simply necessary information.

Weave Exposition into the Story

Because exposition isn't the story, use it sparingly and, best of all, intermittently. Not in large chunks. Weaving the exposition into the story in small amounts is a definite aid to pacing: it allows the reader to grasp the salient information quickly without coming out of the story.

In chapter one of *Sound Proof* I wove all of the above exposition into the story in small pieces (seldom even a full sentence long), so that the reader would not come out of the story at any point.

Here, in its entirety, is chapter one from *Sound Proof,* with the exposition in boldface. As you can see, I don't make the reader wade through paragraphs of exposition: I intertwine it with Frank's thoughts and what's happening in the story. This approach helps hold reader interest because the forward movement of the story isn't halted. Woven-in exposition improves the pacing of the novel.

1 Monday

Shelby Stubbs stepped onto a bale of straw and looked down on the group of musicians. I leaned against a porch rail and watched everything in sight. Even Stubbs, though he wasn't the thief.

Stubbs hooked a thumb through his belt, puffed out his chest, and repeated his announcement. "No sir. Absolutely not." This was directed at Vance Jurasek, who was balancing a string bass on its endpin. "Only fiddles, guitars, and banjos," Stubbs lectured. "No other instruments allowed. That's 'cause no other instruments belong."

"You're kidding." Jurasek settled his bass against the rail and scowled.

"No sir. You don't see a bass in old-time music. It's not traditional. You never saw an old-time player carrying a bass around. No bass in my class."

Jurasek, his thin ponytail hanging limp in the prairie heat, waved a small emerald-green instrument bag at Stubbs. "You'll accept a mandolin, though, right? Bill Monroe played the mandolin."

Stubbs glared. "Don't tell me what Bill Monroe played. I don't dispute that mandolins have a fine sound. Fine for bluegrass. But they don't belong in old-time music. 'Sides, I heard you playing that mandolin as we drove in, and either you or the instrument is off key."

Face flushed, Jurasek shot Stubbs a murderous look.

My eyes scanned the two dozen people agape at Stubbs' announcement. Ranging in age from late teens to early seventies, they had one thing in common: folk music. Make that two things: folk music and T-shirts that advertised the festivals they'd already attended: Augusta

Heritage, John C. Campbell Folk School, Summer Solstice, Swannanoa Gathering.

This week they were attending Midwest Music Madness where, based on what happened the two previous years during Old-Time Music Week, at least one of them would have an instrument stolen.

"Waydell Ames would have taught us," someone said.

"Waydell's dead," Stubbs retorted.

The bluntness of the remark stopped conversation cold. **Stubbs and his band had been signed as a replacement after Ames had died of a heart attack three weeks earlier.**

Seconds ticked by, then argument started in again. "The hammered dulcimer—"

"No! No big old hammered dulcimers. The sound is much too rinky-tink, it just piddles around in the high end. A hammered dulcimer can't drive the music." Stubbs pointed a finger at the dulcimer player. "Only a fiddle can drive the music."

I glanced at the name tag of the musician who had just spoken. Guy Dufour, Maine. Sensing my scrutiny, he turned and **stared at my tag in return, seeing Frank Dragovic, Chicago.** Dufour's name tag didn't identify which instrument he played. **Mine didn't identify me as a private eye.**

"Hammered dulcimers play in old-time music band all over New England." Dufour shouldered two large gig bags easily. Maybe back in Maine he was a lumberjack. **Didn't matter, because I wasn't here to watch him.**

"That's contra dance, not old-time," Stubbs barked, wiping the sweat off his forehead with a yellow bandana.

Not even 9 A.M. in downstate Illinois and the temperature had allemanded past 90° and was eager to do-si-do with 95°. Sweat percolated down my neck and into my White Sox T-shirt.

"Hammered dulcimer in a contra band is fine if you can get a good player. But it ain't an old-time instrument."

On the opposite side of the porch, Kofi Quay and Booker Hayes leaned against a rail. Quay held an African drum and observed; Hayes softly plucked a banjo and grimaced. If they were pondering the antics of white folks, I couldn't blame them.

"Nothing in the literature excluded other instruments," Dufour insisted. "I paid my money, I am going to take your class."

Sneering at the word literature, Stubbs patted back his salt-and-pepper hair and hitched up his pants. He breathed deeply, his belly stretching out his dark blue T-shirt. Any Old-Time You Wanna, it offered. Unlike most of us, who wore shorts to fight off the heat, Stubbs — who had not arrived Sunday night with everybody else, but during breakfast this morning — wore chinos. "Old-time music is fiddle, guitar, and banjo," he reiterated from his wobbly pulpit. "The fiddle plays the melody, the guitar holds down the rhythm, and the banjo fills in. That's the way it is." He looked down at the group. "I'll be touring France later this year, and that's what I'll be taking with me — my fiddle, a guitar player, and a banjo player."

"What about autoharps?" asked Jurasek angrily. Standing with his left side facing Stubbs, the better to see him, he removed a minidisc player from his pocket and flipped it open. Jurasek's right eye was glass. Last night he'd worn a black patch, this morning he didn't. **He was one of those I was here to watch.** I looked around to see if he carried an autoharp in addition to his bass and mandolin. Apparently not.

"Autoharps are for ladies who like to strum and pluck. So are mountain dulcimers."

The sound of a vehicle driving over gravel made me glance left. An old blue Ford pickup bounced across the parking lot. A nylon tarp covered what I surmised was camping equipment and an instrument or two. From the dining hall behind us plates and silverware clattered. People ambled by on their way to class, staring at Stubbs on his bale of straw. Under a massive sycamore tree a boy of about ten practiced "The Battle of New Orleans" on his guitar. To my untrained ear, he sounded good.

The group around Stubbs milled restlessly, its din reaching crescendo.

"I will come to your class," repeated Dufour, who was dressed in a long-sleeved shirt, jeans, and heavy boots. July in Maine must be a nippy month. I wondered if he'd make it through a hot and humid week in the Midwest.

Craning his neck, Stubbs studied Dufour's second bag. "What've you got in there — a pregnant mandolin?"

"I build and play the hurdy-gurdy."

"Ohhhh!" wailed Stubbs, throwing back his arms in mock despair. "The hurdy-gurdy is nothing but a substitute for bagpipes. Now if you like bagpipes, you have another problem."

I felt a finger tap my arm. "What's happening?" whispered **Suzanne, the main reason I was here.**

"Madness," I whispered back.

Mary Ployd, the organizer of Midwest Music Madness, and my employer for the week, emerged from the breakfast area, winding a thick guitar strap around one hand. "What's going on here?" she demanded.

"He's telling us we can't take his class. We signed up and paid our money and he's telling us we can't take his class." **Lafayette Wafer** bounced up and down in indignation. **He was another one to watch.** "I paid to play the bowed psaltry in Waydell's class, and now Shelby—"

"The bowed psaltry!" roared Stubbs. "I liked it better when you scratched away on that miserable little fiddle of yours, Lafayette. The bowed psaltry ain't even a real instrument! It's a Christmas tree gone bad! No instrument — I repeat, no instrument — deserves to be in a class with a bowed psaltry." He shuddered dramatically. "Compared to that thing, the hurdy-gurdy sounds good."

Mary pushed her way through the group. "Shelby," she questioned, "are you trying to exclude these students from your class?"

Stubbs barely looked at her. "They don't belong in an old-time class, Mary. You should know that."

"What are you talking about?" she demanded, swinging a long braid of brown hair over her back. Her voice lowered. "You signed a contract to teach old-time ensemble. I sent you a list of twenty-five students, with the instruments they played. Our agreement was that you teach them."

"That's right!" shouted Lafayette Wafer in a reedy voice. Mary scowled at him over her shoulder.

Stubbs shook his head. "Didn't get no such list. Wouldn't have agreed to it if I had."

Mary unwrapped the web strap from one hand and wrapped it around the palm of the other, like surgical tape. Or brass knuckles. "Be that as it may, you signed the contract, the students paid their money, and the best thing for everybody is that you accept them into your class. Next time, I'll make it clear that only fiddle, guitar, and banjo are permitted in your class." From the way she looked at Stubbs, I doubted there would be a next time.

He shook his head. Avoiding eye contact with Mary, he gazed out over the heads of those gathered on the porch.

"Let's go to my office and discuss this." She turned to go.

"No."

She turned back to Stubbs. Unwrapped the strap from her hand. Clipped it around her waist. "It would be better if we discussed this in private. We're upsetting everybody out here."

"I am not upset," shouted Dufour. "Nobody can keep me out of the class I signed up for."

Mary turned in a circle. Caught my eye. I half-expected a sign that she wanted my help. **Dealing with big-headed musicians wasn't what she hired me for, and I didn't think she wanted me to blow my cover,** but I was willing to drive a charge against Shelby Stubbs if that's what she wanted.

No sign came.

"Shelby," said Mary softly. "Please step down from that bale."

He considered it. After a moment, he acquiesced.

"I want you to think about this." She touched his arm. He flinched. "This is the kind of thing you could end up regretting. Imagine driving along on a dark, rainy night. Twisty roads, nobody in sight. Fog everywhere. The kind of night that makes you look back on your life, you know?"

Stubbs stared at her.

"There you'd be, all lonesome and sad, just you and the dark and the rain. What would you be thinking? I know you'd be wishing you could do things over. This would be something you'd wish you had done different." She paused. "But then it would be too late."

I stared at Mary, whose words carried an overtone of threat.

Stubbs cleared his throat.

"So do the right thing now, Shelby. Teach these students what you know about old-time music."

Nobody spoke. Sensing her advantage, Mary pushed on. "Half of them — more than half — didn't sign up until they heard you were going to be here. They came because of you, Shelby. They aren't beginners, they're all advanced students, and they want to take a master's class from you." Again she paused. "Please don't disappoint them."

Stubbs worked his jaw. "It ain't right," he croaked. "It's against my principles."

I heard Mary grit her teeth. Sounded like four-four time to me. "I understand that," she soothed. "But what if you didn't do it for yourself? What if you dedicated this class to Waydell's memory? An honorable gesture from one musician to another."

Stubbs shifted from one foot to the other.

"You knew Waydell long ago. Played with him way back then."

A truck door slammed. Stubbs jumped as if he'd been stabbed with a psaltry bow.

"All right," he grumbled. "All right. I'll do it. Just this once."

"Good," said Mary.

Good?

I had my doubts. *Ako laze koza, ne laze rog.* A Croatian saying my mother is fond of repeating. *If the goat lies, its horns don't.*

Wafer and a few others picked up their instruments and headed toward the barn. Jurasek balked. "I'm not taking his class! The son of a pup is closed-minded and musically unimaginative."

Not saying son of a bitch struck me as prudish, if not closed-minded and verbally unimaginative, but I wasn't here to spice up anyone's expletives.

Mary pushed Jurasek in front of her, back toward the farmhouse. "You can take my class, Vance. You'll be a welcome addition, with your knowledge of music."

I turned to Suzanne, who I had met when she came to me with a case last October. I wanted us to live together, but she wasn't saying yes. "You were right," I said to her. "It won't be dull."

Behind us, somebody tolled the bell. Suzanne hurried off to her morning class, **as did the other 200 or so students.** I strapped on my tool belt and headed toward the barn. **For this particular gig, I was undercover as a carpenter.**

Avoid Putting Exposition into Dialogue

Exposition is usually best handled in narrative, not in dialogue. Many beginning writers (and even experienced ones) make the mistake of putting exposition into dialogue in such a way that characters are telling each other things they each know the other knows. Such scenes are very jarring for the reader, who understands that people in real life don't talk that way.

Here's an example of bad exposition, made up for the purposes of this book. In other words, this example does not exist in *Sound Proof.*

"You told me Mary Ployd had been your babysitter," I said to Suzanne.

"Um-hmm," Suzanne agreed. "From the time I was six until I was almost twelve. That's why I want you to help her by finding out who's stealing instruments."

"Not an easy job," I said. "Not with 200 musicians roaming around the farm at all hours of the day and night. And not while I'm working undercover as a carpenter, the way Mary wants me to."

You can tell that the above dialogue has no purpose other than to give pre-story information to the reader. Frank and Suzanne both already know the things they're saying to one another. As you will recall from the chapter on scenes, good dialogue serves three purposes: to reveal character, to show conflict, and to move the story forward. The sample exposition-laden dialogue does none of these.

Beginnings

In her book *Beginnings, Middles, and Ends* Nancy Kress defines the beginning as the first two chapters of the novel. I've always thought this was an accurate assessment, though in some cases the beginning can be just the first chapter. Whether your beginning is one, two, or three chapters long, its job is to draw the reader into the story so that he wants to know what happens next. Ever since the days of Greek drama, readers have been drawn into a story that starts *in medias res:* in the midst of things.

Writers probably spend more time writing and rewriting the first two chapters of their novels than they spend on the rest of the novel in total. (That's good and bad. Good that a lot of time is spent on the beginning of the story. Bad that not enough time is spent on the middle and end of the story.) Many writers, beginning or experienced, have the tendency to start telling themselves the story as they start writing. (I've done this, and sometimes still do it.) That is, they're figuring out what happened before the story starts, and they write it as exposition. Or maybe they even start out with a flashback. Or prologue. And then they need to find a way to get rid of all this clutter and get to the heart of the story: the part the reader wants to hear.

Writing a novel is difficult work. The story in one's head and heart doesn't translate to the page easily. When I start writing a new book I almost always write the first two or three chapters and then, once I see what kind of story I'm writing, I go back and rewrite these first chapters until they feel right to me. Often, this means I delete the second chapter altogether, keeping only the first and third. (In first drafts I have a tendency to put all my exposition and backstory into the second chapter.)

This is exactly what happened with *Sound Proof*. The original second chapter was a meeting between Frank, Suzanne, and Mary, in a bar in Chicago. Mary told Frank her story and asked him for help. This felt right as I wrote it . . . but not after I re-read the first three chapters. *All* of chapter two was exposition.

Y-A-W-N.

I was doing what writers often do: telling the story to myself so that I could better understand it. It's okay (maybe even inevitable) to do that, as long as you go back and get rid of all the deadwood later: deadwood being the parts that are just exposition or that don't feel vital . . . that bog down the story readers want to hear.

Once you know where your story begins (exactly where, in the midst of things, you want to begin), then the rest will become easier. Once you've nailed your beginning, you can scatter your exposition throughout that beginning in small doses.

Of all the stories I've written, I think that *Sound Proof* has the best *in medias res* beginning. That's because it starts off in the middle of a quarrel Shelby Stubbs is having with his music students. This quarrel reveals Stubbs' character and also reveals the characters of several of his students. (Lafayette Wafer, Guy Dufour, and Vance Jurasek all react in different ways.) The scene also reveals part of Mary Ployd's attitude toward Stubbs. Most importantly, this scene reflects the reasons for the later murder of Stubbs.

In addition, the scene contains at least two important foreshadowings. I'll discuss these in another chapter.

When to Introduce the Villain

When I was a ghostwriter for the Boxcar Children series, I was given a set of instructions that each ghostwriter had to follow. Among the instructions were these two: (1) the villain must be one of the major characters; (2) all major characters must be introduced by the end of the second chapter.

The Boxcar books are ten chapters long, so this means that the villain had to be introduced at least 20% of the way through the book. This made good sense to me in terms of novel construction because the Boxcar series is written at a third-grade reading level, for children aged roughly 7-10. For children this age, it's important that the story be straightforward. No structural tricks. No point-of-view tricks.

About the same time that I was ghostwriting the Boxcar Children mysteries, I began to notice that some writers of adult mysteries (at least, the writers I was reading) were beginning to make villain choices that I found annoying. For instance, in a few books the murderer wasn't introduced as a character until the last 25% of the story. In another, the murderer didn't even have a speaking part! (Talk about a minor-minor character.)

Let me digress a moment to say that I'm deliberately using the word *villain* rather than *antagonist*, because in an adult mystery the antagonist (the person who stands opposed to the protagonist) may not be the villain (the one who committed the crime). In *Sound Proof*, for example, Mary Ployd is the main antagonist. Until the very end, she stands in the way of Frank solving the murder. Mary is the antagonist, but she isn't the villain.

Pushing the Envelope

Adults are generally advanced readers who can comprehend more possibilities than can children, so it's understandable that somebody writing an adult mystery may want to push the envelope, do something that hasn't been done before. It's also understandable that somebody who has written maybe a dozen mysteries with the same protagonist might want to try something different, just to keep from being bored while writing.

But in such a case I think it's far more important to consider reader satisfaction than it is to consider writer amusement. Is a reader going to be satisfied when the villain is withheld from the first 75% of the novel, and is introduced only near the end? I'm not. I don't want to see the detective (and me, the reader) spinning his wheels, trying to solve the problem, when as a reader I don't even know about the existence of the person who turns out to be the villain. Likewise, I would like the villain to be "on the page" and have a speaking part. I'm simply not satisfied with villains who don't appear as characters.

So one of the things you as a writer will have to consider is: when do you introduce the villain? Part of the answer depends on whether your villain is a major character or a minor one. If he's a major character, I think you can wait a while before introducing him — because, once introduced, he may be on the scene often and he may play an important role in the story. The reader will get to know him and possibly suspect him.

If the villain is a minor character, she won't play a big role throughout the story, and you may plan for her to not be present in much of the story. However, I think readers will find more satisfaction with your mystery if they encounter this minor character villain frequently. There are minor characters who are hardly there, and then there are minor characters who are present often. In most cases, it's the latter that you want to develop, so the reader won't feel tricked.

In *Dirty Proof* I didn't introduce the villain until chapter twelve. The novel has twenty-eight chapters, so I introduced the villain, a main character, approximately 40% of the way into the story. If I were to rewrite this story today, I think I'd make efforts to introduce the villain earlier: maybe about 25-30% into the book.

When I started to write *Sound Proof* and knew that my villain was a minor character, I felt I had to compensate for this by having him present often. As you can see in the chart, I have

Presence of Minor Character Villain in *Sound Proof*

Chapter 1 — In a way, yes
Chapter 2 — Yes
Chapter 3 — Yes
Chapter 4 — Yes
Chapter 5 — Yes
Chapter 6 — Yes
            Chapter 7 — No
            Chapter 8 — No
      Chapter 9 — Mentioned
            Chapter 10 — No
            Chapter 11 — No
Chapter 12 — Yes
            Chapter 13 — No
Chapter 14 — Yes
            Chapter 15 — No
            Chapter 16 — No
      Chapter 17 — Mentioned
Chapter 18 — Yes
            Chapter 19 — No
            Chapter 20 — No
            Chapter 21 — No
Chapter 22 — Yes
Chapter 23 — Yes
            Chapter 24 — No
Chapter 25 — Yes
            Chapter 26 — No
Chapter 27 — Yes
Chapter 28 — Yes

the villain present in thirteen of the twenty-eight chapters. In two additional chapters I have Frank Dragovic think about or mention this minor character: that makes a total of fifteen out of the twenty-eight chapters that Glover is present in.

That's 54% of the chapters. I don't think it's an absolute necessity to have a minor character villain present in or mentioned in over 50% of the chapters. But I don't think it hurts, either. My guess is that if you want a minor character to be the villain and you also want to play fair with the reader, that minor character should be present in at least a third of the chapters. Playing fair with the reader is the main point.

If you glance at the "presence" chart again, you can see that the villain is present in the first six chapters. This means that the reader gets to know who this minor character is: he's firmly established in the reader's mind.

Then he comes and goes for a while.

But the last eight chapters reflect the first group: the villain is present in six of these eight chapters. As the climax of the story draws near, I bring Glover back into the story in almost every chapter. That, I hope, makes for a satisfying reader experience.

Finally, chapter eighteen is a pivotal chapter in *Sound Proof*. Much of what happens later is a result of things that happened or that Frank observed in chapter eighteen. I made sure to have the villain present in that chapter, to help tie him to the past and to the motive for murder.

Not only did I have the minor-character villain present in more than half of the *Sound Proof* chapters, I also made sure to use foreshadowing when developing the villain. Foreshadowing is covered in the next chapter.

Foreshadowing

Think of foreshadowing as hinting. To foreshadow an event in a novel is to give earlier hints that it might happen. Great writers such as Shakespeare, Dickens, and Faulkner all use foreshadowing, whose purpose is twofold: to involve the reader more in the story by creating anticipation and suspense, and to make the events to come seem more plausible.

Foreshadowing adds richness, tension, and depth to a story. When the foreshadowed events happen, they feel more profound or important because it appears that some cosmic force had underlined their importance by "warning" us they are to come. It's as if Zeus, looking down from Mount Olympus, takes a giant red pencil and "underlines" certain life events, be they words, actions, or even the weather. This makes it seem that what happens was meant to happen.

Books which lack foreshadowing seem so much more "on the surface" than books in which events are intricately bound to future results through foreshadowing.

Big Events

But if you're thinking that you're required to foresee and insert foreshadowing from the beginning of your story — at a time when you're worrying about character, plot, setting, and dozens of other things — rest assured that foreshadowing is often added during a rewrite. Once you've reached the end of your first draft, you know where your story started, where it ended up, and how it got there. Now's the time to ponder which events you want to foreshadow (to make them more anticipated, and to make them more plausible) and how you want to accomplish that.

Foreshadowing can be obvious or it can be subtle. In most cases, subtle is best. Zeus doesn't want to draw *three* red lines under an event: that's so obvious he may as well send down a thunderbolt. One faint red line is sufficient. Most readers will sense that something is important about this object or these events.

The biggest events of your novel give the most satisfaction if they've been foreshadowed. After I finished the first draft of *Sound Proof* I asked myself which events I wanted to foreshadow. The biggest event of most mysteries is the confrontation between the hero and the villain, and *Sound Proof* is no exception to that. So I definitely wanted to foreshadow the confrontation between Frank and Jeff Glover. I judged that, therefore, I wanted to foreshadow the barn (where the final confrontation takes place) and the life-and-death struggle itself. If you've already read *Sound Proof,* you know that during the climax Jeff Glover uses a knife and Frank Dragovic uses a pitchfork.

Barn Foreshadowing

Let's take the barn first. I foreshadow its importance at the very beginning of chapter two, when Frank is recalling childhood summers on his uncle's farm. He remembers: *Each morning when I woke and looked out my bedroom window, the first thing I saw was the barn. Massive. Permanent.* This is a subtle foreshadowing of the importance of the barn, where the final struggle takes place.

In chapter seven, when Edric English peers into Stubbs' trailer to see why Bliss and Frank are there, he sees Stubbs' lying dead.

> *Holy Christ!"* Edric stared at Stubbs' body. His shock seemed genuine.
> "He's gone to the barn," he said, so low I barely heard him.
> I'd heard the expression before. Understood its weight. Death and barns are serious business. For all the shelter they provide, barns can be deadly places. Within their walls farmers have been gored by bulls, crippled by machinery, or killed by falls out of hay lofts.
> "I've called the sheriff," I told English. "Don't move, you'll contaminate the crime scene."

This foreshadowing isn't as subtle as the first mention of the barn: this one talks about the connection between barns and death.

In chapter fourteen, as the weather begins to change for the worse (almost always a foreshadowing), Frank notices: *Over on the barn a shutter swayed. The weather vane had stopped fishtailing and indicated a steady west wind.* When the storm arrives, everybody takes shelter in the barn. When the storm hits, the barn sways with the fierce winds. And it is in the barn, during the big storm, that Mary goes to pieces, as does Jeff Glover, who plays "The Wind and the Rain" on his fiddle — both of them remembering the event from their past.

Further, the villain's first attempt to kill Mary Ployd is to push her out of the hayloft door of the barn, onto the ground below. The foreshadowing about the importance of the barn was plentiful, but always in small doses. Subtle is better than heavy-handed.

Pitchfork Foreshadowing

As to the pitchfork, it couldn't be a weapon that Frank found handy in the very last chapter. That would be lucky, coincidental, and not very believable. If I were reading such a book, with no mention of the pitchfork until the very moment Frank grasps it in the last chapter, I would think, "Author convenience! Author just put the pitchfork there."

The author can't just put the pitchfork there. She has to work to make it not only probable that the pitchfork was there and that Frank used it, but she also has to make the reader feel that this was inevitable. Further, she has to make it seem plausible that Frank could throw the pitchfork with accurate and deadly aim.

So, although I did have the pitchfork in use throughout the book even as I wrote the first draft, I made sure that I did even more foreshadowing when I rewrote. In fact, I planted the pitchfork in the second chapter (where it hadn't been in the first draft), in the very same paragraph in which Frank is thinking about barns: *Out there on the prairie I learned how to raise soybeans and corn, milk cows and slop hogs, muck manure and bale hay. My sister and I and our cousins built tunnels in the stacked hay and swung from hay trolley ropes.*

When nobody was looking we hurled pitchforks at targets and dueled with scythes.

I brought in the pitchfork again in chapter nine, when ten-year-old Cody Thompson is throwing a pitchfork for fun and Fonnie Sheffler is angry with him for doing so. Frank then takes over:

> I put out my hand and Cody reluctantly turned over the pitchfork.
> "Let's go down by the woods," I said, leading us to a small stand of trees.
> Nothing wrong with wanting to toss a pitchfork javelin-like. I'd done it, my sister had done it, my cousins too. I was just surprised that Cody, being a farm kid, didn't have better technique. I gave him a few pointers, tossed the pitchfork a few times myself.
> "Fonnie's clueless, is she?" I asked.
> "Yeah. Cindy's cool, though. She helped me when I fell from the tree and broke my leg. Jeff's cool, too. He's going to show me how to make bones.
> "Hey, Frank."
> "Yeah?"
> "You're cool, too."
> Cody treated the pitchfork toss as if it were an Olympic event. I left him to his practice and walked back to the farmhouse. I wanted to know who else had died here.

In this foreshadowing I again let the reader know that Frank used to throw pitchforks. I implied that he's pretty good at it (he knows how to teach Cody, and he also is surprised that Cody's not better at it). But then, because I didn't want the foreshadowing to be heavy-handed, I deflected its seriousness by having Frank observe that Cody was treating the pitchfork toss as if it were an Olympic event. When humor is added at the end of a serious situation or observation, it serves to deflect from that situation and, in this case, make the foreshadowing less obvious.

In chapter twenty-two the pitchfork appears again, this time in the hands of Guy Dufour, who's using it to pitch straw. The weapon has now made its way into the barn. And then, toward the end of chapter twenty-two, Cindy carries a pitchfork to the afternoon "appetizer" music class, where she plays it as an instrument. In fact, I mentioned the word "pitchfork" many times at the end of the chapter, and even had Frank wishing he could play the pitchfork.

Six chapters later, at the climax, the pitchfork has been foreshadowed often enough that its presence and use make very satisfying sense:

> "I can slit your throat," Glover explained, "or I can push you out of the barn again. There's no straw down there now. But you still might live. I fell and lived, and you might, too. What do you think?"
> My right hand closed around the hard hickory shaft of the pitchfork. Cindy had left it there, thrust into a bale of straw. I worked it loose.
> Glover heard, jerked in my direction. When Mary pulled away from him, he let her go. She fell to the floor. Pitchfork in hand, I drew back my shoulder.
> "Drop the knife!" I shouted.
> Glover's feet moved, his knife arm went back.
> I hurled the pitchfork.

The important events in your novel must be foreshadowed if you want to increase reader enjoyment through anticipation or suspense. And you create this foreshadowing by adding information in subtle ways when you start rewriting.

Minor Characters

Foreshadowing need not be limited to major events. You can, without being heavy-handed about it, foreshadow anything or anybody you feel needs it. Because the murderer in *Sound Proof* is a minor character, I felt that he and his presence at Midwest Music Madness needed foreshadowing. I did this in order to increase reader enjoyment when the villain is revealed. The reader could reflect on what he had been told about Jeff Glover and see that, yes, there were signs.

For example, in the very first chapter, as Frank is standing on the porch observing Stubbs and the other musicians, he notes: *The sound of a vehicle driving over gravel made me glance left. An old blue Ford pickup bounced across the parking lot. A nylon tarp covered what I surmised was camping equipment and an instrument or two.*

And still in the first chapter, when Mary Ployd is trying to convince Shelby Stubbs to accept "odd" stringed instruments into his class, Frank observes:

> Stubbs shifted from one foot to the other.
> "You knew Waydell long ago. Played with him way back then."
> A truck door slammed. Stubbs jumped as if he'd been stabbed with a psaltry bow.
> "All right," he grumbled. "All right. I'll do it. Just this once."

Stubbs jumping as if he had been stabbed is foreshadowing, though this early in the book the reader won't notice it. It's Jeff Glover who's driving the pickup truck, and it's Jeff who slams the door. It's Jeff Glover who was with Stubbs, Mary, and Waydell on a fateful night decades earlier.

In the second chapter the reader learns that among the many things Glover sells are hand-forged knives. But attention on these knives is quickly replaced by attention on the hand-made wooden bones Glover sells, and the fact that Frank buys a pair for Suzanne.

Again, this kind of foreshadowing is subtle, and most readers won't pick up on it as they read the book for story. But at the end readers will have had a much more satisfying experience than if the foreshadowing hadn't been there. They will remember the foreshadowing (Zeus underlining the cosmic significance of certain events), and/or they will flip backwards through the book, looking for it.

It's your job as a writer to make sure they find what they're looking for — a richer, more satisfying reading experience.

Dialogue

People of all ages (children included) love dialogue, and most writers love to write dialogue. I could even say that most writers *live* to write dialogue. (If you neither love dialogue nor enjoy writing it, your turn will come in the next chapter.) When writers think about their work-in-progress, they often imagine scenes, with characters talking to one another.

Remember that scenes are told in real-time: the action occurs on the page. Scenes are life-like, and it's dialogue that gives them this life-likeness. But in fiction dialogue is even more pared down and intense than in real life.

In fiction, dialogue has a purpose. Let's begin with what its purpose is not. The purpose of dialogue is *not* to show how witty and clever you are. Occasionally writers, wrapped up in love of their own words and wit, proceed as if cleverness were the purpose of dialogue. Until you truly understand and internalize the purpose of dialogue, you will be writing at a disadvantage — not making your scenes as strong as they could be, because you may end up shoving the two main purposes of dialogue into second and third place.

The two main purposes of dialogue are to reveal character (usually through conflict) and to advance the plot. (Remember: the purpose of dialogue is not to provide exposition!)

What Dialogue Reveals

How does dialogue help develop character? Dialogue takes place during scenes, and each scene, as you will recall, contains some sort of conflict, however minor or major. Each person wants something different: a different outcome. The way the characters go about obtaining what they want reveals the stuff they are made of. Their dialogue helps show the relationship between them.

Here's a scene from chapter twenty-two of *Sound Proof*. It

occurs after Mary Ployd has been pushed (even though she denies it) out the hayloft door. Mary is taken away by ambulance and the festival goers are about to start their afternoon classes.

> I walked around to the west side of the barn and up the earthen ramp to the second floor. Bales of hay were stacked nearly to the ceiling for half the depth of the barn. Alongside the hay was the straw, similar from a distance, different up close. The sheriff was in silhouette, lit by the hayloft door.
> Finely milled particles of hay seed and dust covered the century-old floor, imparting a slippery quality to it. I suppose if you weren't careful, you could slide right out the door and forty feet down to the ground. Uncle Rudy had told me stories of people falling out of hayloft doors to their deaths or to a crippled existence. He also told me stories of the lucky cases who landed on the hay below and survived without a scratch.
> I stood beside Davis and looked down.
> "What do you make of the straw down there?" he asked.
> What it looked like was a rummage sale on straw: entire bales, sections of bales, and forked loose straw were all mixed up below. Lots and lots of straw. More straw than the normal person would scatter if asked to cover up a muddy area. "I'd say Vance and Guy enjoyed their work."
> "Yeah," he replied, giving me a look. After a while, he spoke again. "I'd hate to think Mary staged this whole thing. I'd hate to think the two of you are trying to put something over on me."
> I examined the floor, searching for scuff marks, footprints, signs of a struggle. The pine boards were worn through in layers. I worked a few splinters loose with the toe of my shoe. Looking for evidence of a scuffle here was like listening for one drum beat in a thousand.
> "I'm an outsider," I said, "so I can see why you'd want it to be me." He glared at that, but I continued. "What I don't understand is why you want it to be Mary. Sure, she may have said she wanted to kill Stubbs, but that's not enough. Even proposing to you after he was dead isn't enough."
> "It's suspicious."
> I asked if there was something else, something he wasn't telling me. His response was to remind me to leave the murder investigation alone.
> Right.
> "You may not believe this, Dragovic, but I don't

want it to be Mary."

Time to cut to the chase. "I agree with what you said out there. I think somebody pushed her."

"If that's true — who's she protecting?" demanded Davis. "And why, that's what I want to know."

We tossed it around. She fell. She jumped. She was pushed.

"Help me out here," he complained. The sheriff teetered on his toes, back and forth. A bit close to the edge. Maybe he intended to illustrate a point. "If she fell," he said, teetering forward, "then we have to accept it's just a coincidence." He teetered back onto his heels. "Hard to do."

I agreed with that one.

Footsteps sounded on the stairs leading up from the first floor. We turned to see Guy approach, carrying both his dulcimer and hurdy-gurdy. Taking no chances.

"Just the man I wanted to see," said the sheriff, staring hard.

"What?!" demanded Guy, setting down his burden.

"Tell me about the straw down there."

"Mary asked Vance and me to scatter it. Frank was not here or she would have asked him, too. Lafayette tried to help but we sent him away, he almost fell out the door."

"Go on," urged Davis. "Did Mary tell you how she wanted it done?"

Guy shrugged. "She told me the straw and the pitchforks were up here. Lafayette was tired from all the pitchforking, so Vance and I told him to push bales out this door and then we would all go down and scatter them below. He almost went out with one of the bales: I pulled him back. Some of the bales broke open, others did not."

"Why did Mary want this spot covered with straw?"

"It is much frequented," answered Guy with a bored look. "Perhaps she did not want mud in the dining hall or the classrooms."

"How long did you work?" Davis asked.

"We quit at lunch time."

"Did everybody leave here together?"

"Lafayette was already gone," Guy replied. "Vance and I started to leave, but Edric came by to help, and Vance stayed with him. Oh, Cindy was here at the end. She said she would straighten up. Then the vendors came, one by one. I think business was slow after the rain." Looking at his hands, he held them out. "I have blisters already from the pitchfork. So does Vance."

"Why didn't you finish?" asked the sheriff.

"But we did finish!" Guy looked affronted. "We covered the ground. There is no mud. We did a good job." He looked to me for confirmation. I nodded.

"Why didn't you finish scattering the bales that are down there?" asked Davis.

"Oh. That. It would have been a waste," Guy explained. "Mary wouldn't want us to waste the straw." He stepped close to the floor's edge and looked down. "It was easier to get the bales down than it will be to bring them back up, *non?*"

Davis looked Guy up and down, maybe trying to fit him into Edric's shoes and my clothes. As the sheriff was contemplating, Vance Jurasek came walking up the earthen ramp.

"We're here to start working on the gate," Guy said to me. "You have an afternoon class, and Mary said you must take it."

"I thought you were busy running the festival," I commented to Vance.

He dismissed it. "The festival runs itself, except for the office. Kim's there now. The gate seemed important."

"There's wood in the storage shed," said Guy. "What kind of gate do you have in mind?" he asked me.

Davis stood there silently, listening.

I pointed in the direction of the pole barn. "I thought we'd save Mary some money by using timber from the pole barn."

"Good idea." Vance nodded in approval. "Mary loves saving money."

The sheriff snorted.

"*Bon!* We will rescue the wood from the pole barn. This is a magnificent festival," enthused Guy. "The black walnut, the pole barn, so much wood! Mary should have T-shirts made!"

I asked Guy if he wanted me to draw a sketch of the gate, but he assured me he could handle it. "My tool belt's in my car," I told them. "If you need it I'll give you my keys." I looked at my watch.

"I have my own tools," Guy reminded me, "and I still have Jeff's hammer. You'd better run."

Would any detective worth his salt run off to a drumming class instead of investigating?

I'd reserve judgment.

Notice first how the dialogue reveals the relationship between Frank and the Sheriff. On the one hand, the Sheriff treats

Frank as an equal: they are both professional detectives. Frank goes to stand beside the Sheriff. They both look down at the place where Mary landed. The Sheriff asks Frank's opinion: "What do you make of the straw down there?" The Sheriff would not ask this question of anybody else at the festival (except his deputy, who is a very minor character with barely a speaking part). Frank is the only person he would treat this way. The dialogue shows that the Sheriff respects Frank.

Frank's remark, "I'd say Vance and Guy enjoyed their work," is not the answer the Sheriff is looking for. Frank knows it, the Sheriff knows it. The Sheriff wants to know whether Frank thinks the straw that saved Mary's life was put there on purpose . . . possibly directed by Mary herself. What Frank's reply shows is that while Frank knows that he and the Sheriff are both professional detectives, he is not going to help the Sheriff go down the road that implicates Mary Ployd.

Life is full of contradictions, and at the very same time that the Sheriff asks Frank's opinion, he definitely still harbors the suspicion that Mary Ployd is guilty of killing Stubbs. So after Frank's oblique remark, the Sheriff comes to the point: "I'd hate to think Mary staged this whole thing," he says. "I'd hate to think the two of you are trying to put something over on me."

The police seldom, if ever, share such thoughts with civilians: the fact that Yale Davis is sharing these thoughts with Frank shows, once again, respect. But the dialogue also shows that deep down, the Sheriff doesn't want the murderer to be Mary. He's looking for assurance.

Frank doesn't give him this assurance.

Then Guy Dufour climbs the stairs to the hayloft. Immediately the Sheriff begins to question Guy. You can see by the dialogue that the Sheriff does not treat Guy as an equal. You can also see that the Sheriff wants information out of Guy." "Tell me about the straw down there," he commands.

And after that exchange, the Sheriff gets to what is bothering him: "Did Mary tell you how she wanted it done?" he asks. He wants to know if Mary Ployd staged this event by first making sure she would land safely on the scattered straw below.

In the dialogue between the Sheriff and Guy, notice that Yale Davis is a cop through-and-through. One question follows another in rapid succession. He has questions and he wants answers, and the person on the other end had better comply.

Notice two things about Guy Dufour's dialogue. First, he is in no way intimidated by the Sheriff's questions. Because he's innocent, and because he has no idea that Frank and the Sheriff think Mary was either pushed or perhaps faked a fall, he is even bored by the questions, which mean absolutely nothing to him.

Second, notice how Guy's speech pattern indicates either that English is not his first language, or that he's bilingual, or that he's from a region where this type of speech pattern is common. When the Sheriff asks Guy why Mary wanted this particular spot covered with straw, Guy replies: "It is much frequented." That's a slightly odd formulation: a bit formal. The word *frequent* entered the English language in the late Middle Ages, from the French. In fact, the modern-day French word is *fréquent*. Guy Dufour is a French-speaking American from the state of Maine, and I tried to make his dialogue reflect this. Later he uses *non* to end a sentence, in a manner natural to a speaker of French.

Dialogue is more interesting when it reflects the character who's speaking it. Your characters shouldn't speak exactly alike, especially if they come from different social and economic classes and are of different ethnic origins, or from different parts of the country. Just a bit of difference in the speech pattern of a character such as Guy Dufour helps develop his character — one of the two main purposes of dialogue.

Speaking Obliquely

Not only is dialogue best when it reflects the character who's speaking it, not only is it best when it shows the relationship between characters, not only is it best when it indicates the underlying conflict — it's also best when it does so obliquely. That is, indirectly.

In real life people don't speak directly to the point. In fact, some people never speak directly to the point! (Consider politicians, who are masters of circuitous talk.) Likewise in fiction, dialogue has more impact and reveals character better if it's oblique.

Below is a scene from chapter eight of *Sound Proof*. Frank has been sent to find Lafayette and bring him to breakfast. Although obliqueness runs both ways (that is, Frank could speak obliquely and so could Lafayette), for the purpose of example I'm concentrating on Lafayette. Each time that Lafayette speaks obliquely, I've boldfaced the dialogue.

> Psaltry balanced across his bony knees, Lafayette sat cross-legged, dressed in the same clothes he'd worn yesterday. An empty bottle of sherry lay on the dirt beside him.
> "Good morning," I said.
> **"Do you like my playing?"**
> "Uh, the sound attracted me."
> He nodded. "It has that effect on people." He frowned. "*Discerning* people. Not like Shelby Stubbs." He drew the bow across the strings, producing an angry squawk.
> "Were you out here all night?" I asked.
> He plucked a loose hair off the bow. Across his lap lay a second bow. **"The nights are mild."**
> "You spent the whole night here?" Could he have been there at midnight, when I was making my rounds?
> Only if he wasn't playing the psaltry.
> **"A tune was calling me."** He pronounced it with a long-u, *tyoon*. "When a tune calls, I follow."
> "Uh-huh."
> "Listen," he said. "I'll play it for you."
> Before I could demur, he launched into a sprightly number, stroking two bows quickly across the strings. I watched as the bows moved rapidly between the silver pegs. It surprised me that he could sit in a cornfield all night slurping sherry and still compose a brisk tune. I'd been expecting something melancholy.
> The tune was over in no time.
> "Did you like it?"
> "I enjoyed it," I answered truthfully. "What's it called?"
> "I call it 'Mary's Cornfield.'"
> "Mary will love it," I assured him. "In fact, she wants to see you."
> He shook his head.
> I looked at my watch. 7:45 on the dot. Breakfast was being served. My stomach growled. "Why?" I asked.

"Don't you want breakfast, a change of clothes?"

"No."

"What about your class, the old-time ensemble? You wouldn't want to miss Stubbs' class." I watched him carefully.

Not carefully enough — he drew the bow across the strings violently. I refrained from plastering my hands to my ears just in time.

"I was looking forward to that class. Waydell was supposed to teach it." His lips quivered. "But Stubbs insulted me. I don't know why Mary hired him, she never had him before, she doesn't need him now."

"Waydell died," I reminded him.

"Oh." He seemed to be remembering something. **"Waydell. Mary loved Waydell. They went back a long way."**

"Listen, Lafayette: Stubbs is dead."

He looked up at me.

"He died last night. In his trailer." I paused to let that sink in. "When did you last see him?"

Stroking his psaltry, he stared into its sound hole. If a *tyoon* was calling, I didn't hear it.

"Was he at lunch?" Lafayette asked. "I didn't see him at lunch. I looked, because I didn't want to sit near him."

"He wasn't at lunch. Did you see him after drumming class?"

A shake of his head was all the answer I got. He didn't appear interested in Stubbs' death. I remembered something: I hadn't seen Lafayette since the drumming class. "Do you know that somebody stole Guy Dufour's hurdy-gurdy?" I asked.

Another shake of his head.

"That's what the shouting was about — at the end of our drumming class. Remember?"

No response.

"Somebody borrowed my hammer," I tried. "Right after drumming class. Do you know who?"

"Shelby was a bully all his life. He picked on little kids, made fun of them. He took things away from people."

"You grew up with Stubbs?"

"I grew up. He was a bully, always a bully. He took the woman Edric loved." Lafayette pushed himself up, wavered. "I don't want to talk about it anymore. I want breakfast." He zipped his psaltry and bows into a case of tattered black nylon. Clutching it to his chest, he marched unsteadily toward the festival buildings, his chin bobbing.

I picked up the empty sherry bottle and shepherded him to breakfast, sort of like Uncle Rudy's Sheltie used to bring in the woolies.

More than half of Lafayette's dialogue is oblique: he doesn't answer Frank's questions directly, and in some cases not at all. Yet this oblique dialogue more accurately reflects real-life encounters than if you were to have characters speak their thoughts directly, state their goals, hopes, fears, loves, or answer direct questions directly. Readers would soon find that boring. And unreal.

And while it might seem that direct questions and direct answers would move your plot forward, the fact is that obliqueness moves the plot forward in a better manner. Oblique answers cover a lot more ground and imply a lot more than do direct answers. Oblique dialogue enriches your story and thus enriches the reader experience.

Dialogue Advances Plot

The other important job of dialogue is to advance the plot. That is what scenes do, of course, but within each scene the dialogue works to push things forward.

To explain what I mean, let me tell you about a video that's currently (maybe forever) making the rounds on Facebook. It shows a dog and a deer. Between them is a long chain link fence. The dog and deer look at each other and then race each other to the end of the fence. There they pause to see who will start first. One of them does, and off they go again. Over and over. They seem the best of friends and seem to be having great fun.

If this chain link were stretched out for miles and miles, it could represent your plot, beginning at Point A and ending at Point Z. The dog and the deer could race from one end to the other, possibly slowing down at points, possibly jumping obstacles at points. Their actions would be the plot, and when one of them reached the end first, the story would be over.

But the story would be all action: all racing.

And although I'm an action-oriented person, I'm also a person who thinks and reasons, a person who grasps conflict and wants to hear what characters have to say. So I would want the dog and the deer to talk to each other as they raced along the fence. Maybe that dialogue would go something like this:

"Whew! I'm exhausted," said the deer. "Let's get a drink at the stream and take a break." "Ha!" barked the dog as it bounded ahead. "I'm not tired at all. You take the break, and I'll be waiting for you at the finish line." "You'll be sorry," shouted the deer to the departing dog. "You'll exhaust yourself and I'll pass your limp body on my way to the finish line."

This silly conversation reveals conflict: the dog and deer have different attitudes toward the race and even toward how a goal is best accomplished, as well as toward how friendly or unfriendly this particular competition is. The dialogue works to increase the conflict and thus increase tension. In short, the dialogue moves the plot forward by revealing character, motive, and conflict, and by creating reader anticipation.

In conclusion, remember that readers *love* dialogue, and it's your job to give them what they love. Work to make your dialogue as rich and meaningful as possible. Make it witty if that's how you see your characters. Make it oblique for certain. Make it distinct for each character. Do all of this, and you will greatly please your readers.

Description

Description is not voluntary, it is mandatory. As a writer, you develop your setting partly through description. And you develop your characters partly through description. Usually description is put into narrative, but sometimes it can be put into dialogue, as long as it's appropriate to the person speaking. And as long as you must write description, it's best to write it well. This means you need to recognize the difference between bad description and good description.

But first: what is description? Nobody has answered this question better than Rebecca McClanahan, in her book *Word Painting: A Guide to Writing More Descriptively*. I highly recommend this book to all writers, whether or not you admire good description. McClanahan defines description as a "word painting" of the physical aspects of a person, place, or thing. And although we take in a painting with our sense of sight, the fact is that in the world of writing, good description also appeals to the other senses: sound, smell, taste, and touch.

Bad vs. Good Description

I suspect that we've all encountered bad description in our reading. Bad description is an information dump — long paragraphs of description full of details, but the details don't appear to be selected for impact. They're just there, swelling the paragraphs to bursting point, creating the kind of writing that many readers skip in order to "get to the interesting parts."

Information dumps, be they backstory or description, stop the forward movement of the novel. Readers do not want the forward movement of the novel stopped, not for any reason. They want to know what happens next . . . and they don't want to wade through paragraphs of description before they can return to the story.

Bad description, then, usually comes in large chunks. It stops the advancement of the plot. And it often annoys readers, particularly if these chunks appear each time a character meets another or enters a room or drives to a new location.

Good description, on the other hand, does the following:

1) **provides necessary information**
2) **uses selected details for a purpose**
3) **appeals to the senses,**
4) **involves the reader emotionally**
5) **uses language well, often metaphorically.**

I don't consider myself a writer of great descriptions. But setting is very important to me (as described in an early chapter of this book), and so I've trained myself to write description that avoids the pitfalls of bad description.

Early Description in *Sound Proof*

Early in each novel writers supply description: readers need to know where they are and what things look like. In the scene below, from chapter three of *Sound Proof*, Frank is walking around the grounds of Mary Ployd's farm, checking out the musicians, the suspects, and the possible hiding places for stolen instruments. This is before the murder occurs, so Frank is not thinking in terms of murder: if he were, I would have him describe things differently.

> Turquoise, purple, burgundy, yellow, blue — a hundred or more tents bloomed on the camping field like giant wildflowers. Many were inexpensive nylon dome tents with fiberglass poles, the kind anybody could pop up in a couple of minutes. Not the kind you'd want to take on a serious expedition. I peeked into open tents, looking for tarps, boxes, or storage containers of any kind. Lafayette's tent was a scout master's nightmare: three jagged tears on one end, sloppily-tied guy wires, and a mud-spattered front flap. Cindy Ruffo, whose mountain dulcimer had been stolen two years ago at Mary's first Midwest Music Madness, was a seasoned camper. She had even tied pieces of cloth on the guy wires, making

them more visible so people wouldn't trip over them.

I checked out the RVs and campers next, but they were harder to look into. Fonnie Sheffler's grizzled Chesapeake camper was anchored next to Stubbs' Roadtrek, and next to him stood Kim Oberfeld's Chevy truck with a Coleman folding trailer attached to its bed. I lingered a moment at the truck and trailer, then glanced down toward the covered walkway, where Kim still stood behind her vendors table. What Kim lacked that the other suspects had was mobility. So far, she was spending every minute at her table.

From the camper area I reached the recently built cement-block showers, and from there I walked toward the dining hall. When the thief stole his next instrument, he'd have my well-worn path for his getaway.

"Cody Thompson, you watch how you climb." Tansy Thompson, one of the festival's two cooks, stood outside the kitchen squinting up the trunk of a shagbark hickory. As if in reply, a chunk of bark fell from on high.

"He's always climbing," she said, turning to me. "And stay away from the black walnut tree, you hear me, Cody?"

A mumbling from above.

"What's wrong with the black walnut?" I asked.

"Oh," she whispered, "he fell from it the first day of the first Madness. Broke a leg."

Cody scrambled down, swung from the lowest branch, dropped to the ground, came up grinning. He was the guitar-playing ten-year-old. "Can I see Jeff now?" he asked his mother. "He promised to show me his knives. Can I?"

"Yes," she sighed, " but be careful."

Cody was gone before she finished speaking.

"I don't know what these vendors are coming to. That Jeff Glover has knives out on his table. Knives aren't musical instruments."

"Hand-forged," I replied. "I saw quilted purses and vests for sale at one of the tables."

Tansy frowned. We returned to our respective jobs.

My meeting with Mary was scheduled for noon in the farmhouse. An old tractor tire filled with day lilies stood near the back door. The first floor of the farmhouse had been converted to offices. Bedrooms on the second floor housed four instructors: the morning guitar teacher and the afternoon harmonica teacher as well as Raven Hook and Booker Hayes. The third floor constituted Mary's living quarters.

The thermometer on the back stoop read 92°.

Directly under the thermometer, leaning up against the house siding, a nylon instrument case stood unprotected.

I couldn't tell by looking what instrument it housed because the case was long, wedge-shaped and blue — like a Cheesehead after a Green Bay winter.

Lifting the wedge I unzipped it. Inside was a guitar, Tippin by name. A brand I'd never heard of, but I wasn't a musician. Rosewood sides and back, spruce top. Tortoise-shell inlay under the sound hole. Beautiful construction. Worth a few thousand for sure. What was it doing out on the porch in the sizzling heat, at a festival where a thief supposedly picked instruments with the same ease he picked notes? Zipping the case closed, I leaned it against the siding.

Observation with a Purpose

Although there's a lot of description in the paragraphs above (more than I would normally write), the description doesn't stop the advancement of the plot. (Notice that for good pacing I inserted a small scene into the narrative.) The protagonist is in action as he describes: he moves from the tents to the campers to the trees to the outside of the farmhouse, observing as he goes. His observations have a purpose.

Do the descriptive passages here provide necessary information? I think so. They give the reader a visual look at the farm and how it is now full of tents and campers. These details are important to Frank, the detective. The location of the campers turns out to be important to the instrument thefts. Frank's observations about the layout and use of the farmhouse are also important to the plot: Raven's room is just one flight of stairs away from Mary's room. And the blue wedge-shaped guitar case ends up being very important, too.

Note that the details Frank observes and considers in his mind are details that a detective and a carpenter (he is both) would observe. Because Frank knows wood, he knows trees, and he recognizes what kind of woods Mary's guitar is made of. And because he knows construction, he observes and comments on the floor plan of the farmhouse. The descriptions are true to Frank's character.

The descriptions do use selected details for a purpose. Look at this passage again:

> Directly under the thermometer, leaning up against the house siding, a nylon instrument case stood unprotected.
> I couldn't tell by looking what instrument it housed because the case was long, wedge-shaped and blue — like a Cheesehead after a Green Bay winter.

If the details weren't selected for a purpose, the passage might read something like this:

> The back stoop of the farmhouse was small by comparison to the front porch, a mere five feet by three, but covered for protection from the sun and rain. The two concrete steps were well-worn and pitted and the roof newly shingled with what looked like cheap tiles: in keeping with Mary's penny-pinching.
> The large outdoor thermometer, once green but now faded to white, attached to a post with two rusty screws, read 92° — and the day had hardly begun. Directly under the thermometer, leaning up against the faded-gray house siding, a nylon instrument case stood unprotected.
> I couldn't tell by looking what instrument it housed because the case was long, wedge-shaped and blue — like a Cheesehead after a Green Bay winter. A long zipper ran lengthwise around the case. A thick nylon strap was attached to each long end of the case by a black plastic D-hook.

The passage above contains way too many details. So many that they don't appear selected. In fact, they weren't selected: I just blathered on while writing them, describing everything Frank might see. The original passage, however, focuses on those details that are important to the story: the temperature and the blue nylon case.

The sensory details in these passages are almost all visual. That's a weakness: I could and should have brought in some of the other senses. Although immediately following the last sentence, Frank hears a loud grunt, so I do bring sound into the scene. The phrase *well-worn path* might appeal to the sense of touch. Touch is also referred to with the term *sizzling heat*. But, in general, this passage relies on sight, as do most descriptive passages. I vow that the next time I write description, I'll appeal to the other four senses!

Does this description involve the reader emotionally? I hope it does. I worked to achieve emotional involvement, and I did that mainly through Frank's observations. It's easier, or if not easier at least quicker, to involve readers emotionally when you're telling the story from first person POV. Through the details that Frank notices, the reader gets to know Frank better and empathize with him. For example, Frank notices that Lafayette's tent is a mess, and the reader will likely infer that Frank's tent would not be a mess. Likewise, Frank highly approves of Cindy's tent and marked guy wires, and the reader will likely feel that, like Cindy, Frank would take care to protect others from tripping over guy wires.

Figurative Language

Description can come to life when you make a conscious effort to use language well, especially when you employ figures of speech (similes, metaphors, hyperbole, and personification, among others). So that you don't have to flip back and forth between this page and previous ones, I'm reprinting the passage again, with phrases that use language well boldfaced.

Turquoise, purple, burgundy, yellow, blue — a hundred or more **tents bloomed** on the camping field **like giant wildflowers.** Many were inexpensive **nylon dome tents** with **fiberglass poles,** the kind anybody could pop up in a couple of minutes. Not the kind you'd want to take on a serious expedition. I peeked into open tents, looking for tarps, boxes, or storage containers of any kind. Lafayette's tent was a **scout master's nightmare:** three *jagged tears* on one end, sloppily-tied guy wires, and a **mud-spattered front flap.** Cindy Ruffo, whose mountain dulcimer had been stolen two years ago at Mary's first Midwest Music Madness, was a seasoned camper. She had even tied pieces of cloth on the guy wires, making them more visible so people wouldn't trip over them.

I checked out the RVs and campers next, but they were harder to look into. Fonnie Sheffler's **grizzled Chesapeake camper** was anchored next to Stubbs' Roadtrek, and next to him stood Kim Oberfeld's Chevy truck with a Coleman folding trailer attached to its bed. I lingered a moment at the truck and trailer, then glanced down toward the covered walkway, where Kim still stood behind her vendors table. What Kim lacked that the other suspects had was mobility. So far, she was spending every minute at her table.

From the camper area I reached the recently built cement-block showers, and from there I walked toward the dining hall. When the thief stole his next instrument, he'd have my well-worn path for his getaway.

"Cody Thompson, you watch how you climb." Tansy Thompson, one of the festival's two cooks, stood outside the kitchen squinting up the trunk of a shagbark hickory. As if in reply, a **chunk of bark fell from on high.**

"He's always climbing," she said, turning to me. "And stay away from the black walnut tree, you hear me, Cody?"

A mumbling from above.

"What's wrong with the black walnut?" I asked.

"Oh," she whispered, "he fell from it the first day of the first Madness. Broke a leg."

Cody scrambled down, swung from the lowest branch, dropped to the ground, came up grinning. He was the guitar-playing ten-year-old. "Can I see Jeff now?" he asked his mother. "He promised to show me his knives. Can I?"

"Yes," she sighed, " but be careful."

Cody was gone before she finished speaking.

"I don't know what these vendors are coming to. That Jeff Glover has knives out on his table. Knives aren't musical instruments."

"Hand-forged," I replied. "I saw quilted purses and vests for sale at one of the tables."

Tansy frowned. We returned to our respective jobs.

My meeting with Mary was scheduled for noon in the farmhouse. An old tractor tire filled with day lilies stood near the back door. The first floor of the farmhouse had been converted to offices. Bedrooms on the second floor housed four instructors: the morning guitar teacher and the afternoon harmonica teacher as well as Raven Hook and Booker Hayes. The third floor constituted Mary's living quarters.

The thermometer on the back stoop read 92°.

Directly under the thermometer, leaning up against the house siding, a nylon instrument case stood unprotected.

I couldn't tell by looking what instrument it housed because **the case was long, wedge-shaped and blue — like a Cheesehead after a Green Bay winter.**

Lifting the wedge I unzipped it. Inside was a guitar, Tippin by name. A brand I'd never heard of, but I wasn't a musician. **Rosewood sides and back, spruce top. Tortoise-shell inlay under the sound hole.** Beautiful construction. Worth a few thousand for sure. What was it doing out on the porch in the sizzling heat, at a festival where a thief supposedly picked instruments with the same ease he picked notes? Zipping the case closed, I leaned it against the siding.

The boldfaced words indicate a few of the instances in which I used exact nouns, strong verbs, and/or figurative language. For example, *tents bloomed*. Tents do not bloom, but they are being compared to giant wildflowers, which do bloom. And instead of describing Fonnie's camper as *old* or *beat-up* I describe it as *grizzled*: a less common word, a stronger word. Throughout the story I have Frank think in metaphors, usually humorous. This selection includes one example: he compares the blue instrument case to a Cheesehead (self-designated term for Green Bay Packer fans) after a very cold winter. (The "very cold" is unstated, but Green Bay is known for its cold winters.)

In conclusion, recognize that writing description is mandatory: you can't get away with not doing it. Readers want to experience your book emotionally, and some of their emotions will come from well-written description. Likewise, recognize that writing description is a bit like dropping clues — it's better to spread the description throughout the book than to drop it on readers as if you're operating a crane and they're the landing spot for a construction-sized load of lumber.

Readers won't mind (and may even enjoy) paragraphs of description if those paragraphs don't stop cold the advancement of the plot or the development of character. The paragraphs I've reproduced in this chapter describe, but at the same time they advance the plot and develop character.

Solution and Denouement

How many times have you read and thoroughly enjoyed a novel — up until the ending, which you found unsatisfying? If you've never had that experience, you are a rare and lucky reader: most readers have experienced, to one degree or another, disappointments in the way some novels end. This dissatisfaction usually stems from the solution to the crime, though now and then it stems from the denouement. And woe to the writer whose readers are dissatisfied with both the solution and the denouement: these readers may not come back for the next novel.

Writing a good solution to your mystery involves being certain about the protagonist, the villain, the clues you've planted, and the tone of your book.

Know Your Protagonist

Let's start with the protagonist. My guess is that most writers know their protagonist well, and will not write a solution that's false to his or her character. But even the best of writers occasionally slip and end up with a solution (perhaps one that comes to them at the very end, instead of one that they've thought about beforehand) that feels false for the protagonist. As a reader I'm disappointed with solutions in which the hero appears to have overlooked an obvious suspect: a suspect who turns out to corner the hero at the end, threatening his or her life. Each time this happens (the protagonist overlooks an obvious suspect who turns out to be the villain), I feel as if I'm reading a cliche. That is, it seems that the writer feels compelled to put the hero in danger at the end and can think of no better way to do this than to make the hero (and reader) overlook the obvious.

Such a solution may fit the book if you're writing about a protagonist who consistently overlooks the obvious. Then the ending would be organic and satisfying. Such an ending might even be satisfying if only one of the two cliched elements were present: either your hero overlooks an obvious suspect, or a suspect entraps your hero as the book nears its climax. But not both.

Know Your Villains

Likewise, to write a satisfying solution, you need to know your villain well and have him act accordingly. I recently read a novel in a series by a writer whom I admire, but in this particular book the solution didn't work for me because of the villain. She was present throughout the book, in a minor-character sort of way, and that part was fine. But when at the end she reached into her purse, took out a gun, and shot the hero, I was not satisfied. Not at all. What it would have taken for me to be satisfied with this solution was a few subtle hints here and there that this villain carried a gun and was willing to kill people. In short, I needed this event to be foreshadowed. To write satisfying solutions, don't have your villain act in a manner that you haven't prepared the reader for, however subtly.

A corollary to unexpected villains, or their unexpected actions, is the too-obvious villain. If, when you ask critique group members or others to read your manuscript, they all say they knew who the villain was a third of the way through the book, then your solution won't be satisfying because the villain is too obvious. In such a case, you have to ask yourself two questions: (a) can you, through rewriting, make the villain much less obvious? or, (b) should you choose another villain altogether?

In *Dirty Proof* I changed the villain three times. The first time through, everybody who critiqued the manuscript said the murderer was way too obvious. So I changed which character was the villain. In the second set of critiques, readers said the murderer became obvious about two-thirds of the way through the book, and they didn't find his motive satisfying. With the third rewrite, critiques found the villain difficult (but not impossible) to discern, and were satisfied with the resolution. Don't be afraid to change villains.

In a previous chapter I talked about the planting of clues.

If you've done it right (planted enough of them) readers will be satisfied even if they haven't guessed the identity of the villain. They'll be satisfied because, once the identity is revealed, they will understand instantly that, yes, this makes sense: they will have internalized all the clues. If, on the other hand, you haven't planted sufficient clues, or strong enough clues, your readers will say, *What??* They won't understand. And they won't be satisfied.

The Tone of Your Book

Finally, your solution is more satisfying when it's true to the tone of your book. Most solutions are. But more and more (possibly due to pressure from publishers), writers seem to be ending mysteries with thriller-like shootouts. Or explosions. Or chases. These pull-out-all-the-stops endings work only if they fit the tone of what came before in the book. In a thriller they often do fit the tone of what came before. But most mysteries don't have the same tone as do thrillers, so the big-bang endings feel unconnected to everything that came before.

Respect the tone of your book, be it farce, comedy, high-stakes action, classic private eye, police procedural, had-I-but-known amateur detective, or something else. If you're serving your guests a fluffy-looking coconut-covered layer cake, don't add a hidden bottom layer of hard peanut brittle. And if you insist on that hard peanut brittle ending, let your guests know ahead of time — before they break their teeth.

Revealing the Solution

How the solution to your mystery is revealed is almost as important as *what* that solution is. In general the solution will be revealed either through words or through action, or through a combination of the two. In the earliest European and American mystery short stories, the solution was revealed through words: the detective explained. This is also true of the Sherlock stories: the consulting detective, he of the superior intellect, explains to his companions (and thus to the reader) how he reached the solution he did. And readers are satisfied because everything fits together.

During the Golden Age the mystery form was so popular that both writers and critics came up with "rules" for the mystery. All of these rules included playing fair with the reader. Many mysteries of the Golden Age were set in mansions. When it came time for the solution, the detective, sometimes with the aid of police and sometimes not, would call all the suspects into the drawing room and explain, step by step, his reasoning. Then he would name the killer. This, too, is revealing a solution through words.

Sometimes the killer would jump up and try to escape, or would brandish a weapon, only to be subdued. This is revelation through words and action.

But around the time of World War II, mysteries changed. With writers Dashiell Hammett and Raymond Chandler, the hard-boiled detective entered the scene. In these novels the solution is often revealed by action: by a confrontation between the protagonist and villain.

Today most readers aren't satisfied with a drawing-room solution in which the detective calls in the suspects and explains her or his reasoning, then names the guilty party. Such solutions are far removed from our daily experience and from the movies we watch. This doesn't mean that you might not be able to pull off a gather-the-suspects type ending. And if you're writing a period piece, set in another century, the explanation-by-words ending might work best.

Assuming you're writing a modern mystery, though, you will most likely use a combination of action and words in the solution. If that's the case, work to make both the action and the words believable (within the context of the novel). For example, here's the solution (climax) to *Sound Proof*.

> Step after step, stride after stride, oblivious to the danger, she marched up the gravel-covered hill, her clogs crunching loudly. I surged to my knees and knuckles like a sprinter, ready to take off.
> She reached the top and I raced across the grass. At the base of the ramp I shifted right, stepping on the old stone blocks that embanked the dirt. Less gravel there, less chance for sound.

At the top, I paused, listening.

"Who's there?" asked Mary.

But she was facing inward, not in my direction. I stepped on the gravel. Careful, careful. Moved toward the door.

"Who's there?" she repeated angrily. "I saw your light."

As she spoke I slipped through the open doors and flattened myself against the stacked bales of straw, arms flat, head back, listening.

"*Mary!*"

A whisper. I didn't quite recognize the voice. Where was it coming from?

"*Mary!*"

She looked to her left. The granary? The loft above?

The stairs below. A head appeared. Shoulders, chest. The sheriff stood there, gun drawn.

"What are you doing here?" she asked in a normal voice.

"Get out of here," he whispered, "before you get hurt."

"Hurt? What are you talking about?"

"There's somebody here," whispered Davis. "Get out!"

She stood there frozen.

I had no weapon. I looked around in the dark for an implement, a tool, something. I inched closer along the straw.

"Yale, I don't understand." Her voice cracked.

The sheriff moved toward her.

Fell face down, the gun flying from his hand, skittering across the floor toward the granary. Twenty, twenty-five feet away. To reach it I'd have to cross the open door, the moonlight behind me.

Too far.

Mary gasped.

Glover stood there, a club in his hand. Glover — the one who stole my hammer when I raced out of the drumming class.

"You— you— you're . . . ." Mary stopped herself in time.

"Yes. I'm the guy you left to die," he finished. "I'm Bram Bailey."

"You pushed me," she said. "You tried to kill me."

He moved toward her, she stepped back. "You left me for dead, Mary Ployd. Stubbs pushed me off the mountain and you drove away with him."

"But I— he— Oh! You murdered Shelby! You—

you can't get away with this. The sheriff knows. He's not dead. His deputy knows. Frank Dragovic knows. Suzanne knows, Lafayette knows." She was desperate, making up lies wholesale. "Get away while you can, go now."

Glover shook his head, grabbed Mary by the bandaged arm. She cried out in pain and pulled back, but he held on. Dropping the club he pulled out a knife. Long, wide blade, thick shaft. I could rush him, but he could slit Mary's throat in half the time it'd take me to reach him.

"Waydell lied for you," Glover said, holding her close. "He saved my life, you know. When I got better, I went to see him, asked him about Stubbs and you. I think he knew I wanted revenge. Not for myself, a fight's a fight, I didn't hold a grudge for that. It was the fiddle — you know he ran over it deliberately. Waydell told me your name was Mary Ames, said you were his sister and that if any harm ever came to you, I was dead. I believed him."

"Waydell has a sister. Mary."

Glover chuckled. "I know. That's what had me confused for so long. His sister Mary. I assumed she was the one. I never looked her up. If I had, I'd have known she wasn't you. Never mind, though. I waited. It was Stubbs I waited for, and he's dead now."

"You killed him," said Mary needlessly.

"Smashed his head in. Fitting, don't you think, breaking his skull? Bone for bone — my left leg was shattered when he pushed me over the mountain. I heard him the day I drove in, standing on the porch ranting about purity of old-time music. He'd have done better to think of purity of behavior. He was jealous of my playing, wasn't he? He ran over my fiddle deliberately."

"Yes," whispered Mary. "He did. But I didn't. I left Shelby, you know that."

"Bram Bailey," he continued, listening only to himself. "BB. Best Bones. I changed my name so I could kill Stubbs some day, but I kept my initials on my bones. Every time I made a pair, I thought of standing behind him, slipping one over his head, and pulling against his windpipe."

Mary struggled. Glover gripped her more firmly.

With his free hand he held up the knife as if studying it. "But choking him with bones would have brought suspicion on me. Instead, I used what was handy."

Again Mary tried pulling away, again Glover held on.

I edged closer. My hand touched something hard.

"I sang when he was dead, you know," Glover continued. "I went out and sat behind the pole barn and sang rock songs. He knew his time had come when he first saw me — when he wanted to buy my fiddle. That's why he fell over, because he knew I was here for justice."

"You don't have to do this," Mary argued. "Go away, just go away. You can change your name again, I won't tell. I haven't told anybody."

Glover nodded in a distracted way, examining the point of his knife.

"It's your own fault," he said. "I didn't know it was you, that you were the Mary who was with Stubbs. But the night of the thunderstorm, when I was playing my song, you asked the carpenter to have me stop playing and singing. And then I crept close and heard you talking to him about being a singer with Waydell and Stubbs. About playing in the Boot Jacks. That's when I knew it was you, that Waydell had lied."

"He knows," Mary said. "Frank knows it's you! He's not a carpenter, he's a private investigator. I hired him. He'll find you. You can't get away."

Glover ignored her, holding the knife up to her face. "You weren't as bad as he was. I'm going to give you a choice, Mary."

Silence.

"What?" she asked at last.

"I can slit your throat," Glover explained, "or I can push you out of the barn again. There's no straw down there now. But you still might live. I fell and lived, and you might, too. What do you think?"

My right hand closed around the hard hickory shaft of the pitchfork. Cindy had left it there, thrust into a bale of straw. I worked it loose.

Glover heard, jerked in my direction. When Mary pulled away from him, he let her go. She fell to the floor. Pitchfork in hand, I drew back my shoulder.

"Drop the knife!" I shouted.

Glover's feet moved, his knife arm went back.

I hurled the pitchfork.

Climax of *Sound Proof*

In *Sound Proof* the solution/climax takes up approximately four or five pages of a 265-page novel. It comes up fast, just as the music festival is all but over: just as Frank thinks Mary Ployd is safe. The climax of a novel should reach the heights that have been promised throughout the book: in this case, a matter of life and death. The climax of a novel should be short: that's what climaxes are. Mountain peaks are sharp: they are not buttes, where you can build entire towns. When you reach the climax of your novel, reveal it in dramatic ways that increase tension to the utmost. A five-page climax is better than a twenty-page climax. In fact, I doubt that twenty pages constitute a climax because it's too difficult to sustain tension for that long.

Note also that the solution is revealed through a combination of talk and action. But in the case of *Sound Proof* the talk is *not* between the villain and protagonist. One of the reasons for this is that I find the idea of a killer confessing to the detective not very believable: he or she would be smarter to say nothing. And even if the killer intends to confess and then murder the detective, the killer is still better off doing it rather than talking about it. So I don't find killer-revealing-all-to-detective endings that satisfying.

Yet I don't find after-the-fact explanations satisfying, either. If Frank and Glover had simply confronted one another at the end, knife versus pitchfork, with few words spoken, and then Frank explained all that evening — how dull. Too short a climax, too long an explanation.

However, readers need explanations for satisfaction. And so do writers. So I created a climax with three people: protagonist, villain, and intended victim (who in this case is also the antagonist). It made sense to me that Glover would explain everything to Mary before he offers her the choice between the knife and the jump, because he wants her to fully understand what Stubbs did to him and why he feels justified in murdering Stubbs. And her.

It also makes sense to me that Frank, in trying to save Mary's life, would not make his presence known until the very minute he must act. A combination of explanation and action work best, in my opinion, to create a satisfying ending.

Denouement

Having dealt with solution and climax, we come to denouement. Mark Twain called denouement "the marryin' and the buryin.'" It's the final part of the story, where all the strands are woven together.

When writing your denouement, think about what needs to be resolved, and resolve it. Don't elaborate. Denouements are best when they're short: one, two, or three pages. Some writers get so excited by explaining everything that happened or will happen that they end up writing fifteen or twenty-page denouements. For many readers such denouements detract from the feeling of satisfaction with the story. The story is what the previous 250-or-so pages have been about. The story has reached its climax. Give readers a chance to enjoy that climax and savor everything that has happened: don't delay or dilute their pleasure by making them read a long denouement.

The denouement in *Sound Proof* is almost four pages long. That's longer than I like to write denouements, but I had to wrap up an entire music festival, and I think my denouement does its job efficiently. Strive for a short denouement that wraps up the loose ends of the story and leaves the reader very satisfied.

23 Outlining

You may wonder why I've placed a chapter on outlining near the end of this book rather than near the beginning. Isn't outlining something you do before you start writing the novel? And: can you get away without creating an outline? The answers are *Yes* and *Yes, but your job will be much more difficult.*

This chapter is near the end of the book because you shouldn't waste your time creating an outline until after you've considered most of the things I've written about in previous chapters. Certainly you need to think through your initial ideas on plot, characters, setting, conflict, point of view, and subplots before you begin an outline.

As to whether you can get away without first writing an outline, you can. But writing your novel without an outline will be more difficult than writing it with an outline. When you peruse an outline, inspecting it for any problems (plot, subplot, motivation, etc.), you will find that it's much easier to correct an outline than it is to encounter and correct the problem as you're writing the manuscript itself.

When you encounter a problem in the outline (say, for example, you realize that the villain is hardly present in the book at all) it's easier to go back and insert a correction in different parts of the outline than it is to suddenly realize, at the end of your first draft, that you haven't done something you needed to be doing all along: inserting the villain throughout the story. Because outlines are short and basic (in comparison to the novel itself), it's often easier to spot *big* problems within the outline. And it's definitely easier to correct them within the outline, so that your actual writing will avoid these pitfalls.

Outlines need not be long, though there's nothing wrong with writing a long outline . . . as long as you don't use writing the outline as an excuse to avoid writing the book itself. My outline for *She's on First,* my first novel, was short, but it was sufficient for me to "see" the entire book and how the story would develop. My outline for *Sound Proof* was more detailed. I'm not sure why that is: it could be that the plotting of mysteries is more intricate and therefore I wanted more details in the outline. Or it could be that because I was dealing with a large cast of characters, I felt more confident controlling them within an outline.

Neither of my outlines looks like the classic outline format, with Roman numerals and capital letters and lower case numerals and lower-case letters and so on. I find that type of outline stifling: it's as if the form, and not the content, is what's important. I prefer to concentrate on content, and so I use whatever form of outline works for me.

Here is the working outline I used to write *She's on First*. The bulleted lines indicate changes I made after I analyzed my original outline.

Working Outline, *She's on First*

1) THE SCOUT
Curry sits on bleachers watches Linda
play college ball   **POV Curry**
Flashback — to Little League game and
Big Al, same conflict as above   **POV Curry**

2) ON DECK
Linda and Curry in plane to Chicago   **POV Linda**
Eagles office, she meets Al Mowerinski,
asks him why he's drafting her   **POV Linda**
Linda discusses signing
with her parents   **POV Linda**

3) BUSH LEAGUE
Minor leagues, first year, meets
Neal Vanderlin, reporter   **POV Linda**
Conflicts in minors, fan and player
friendliness and hostility, manager
hostility, threats   **POV Linda**

4) AT BAT
Opening Day, what fans are saying, article	**POV Neal**
Opening Day	**POV Curry**
Threat of strike, Al's office, Isemonger ringleader	**POV Al**
On field, Linda, big error first game	**POV Linda**

5) BALK
Manager puts Linda in left field	**POV Neal**
Conflict on team, sexual and racial	**POV Linda**
Same conflict	**POV Al**
Road trip to Frisco	**POV Neal**

6) HIT AND RUN
Isemonger attacks Linda	**POV Linda**
Al fines both	**POV Al**
Flashback — Al, Curry, and Amanda	
• split flashback into 2 or 3 scenes to increase suspense	**POV Al**
• add scene in Al's office, Linda and Isemonger	**POV Linda**

7) DOUBLE PLAY
Team is starting to win, strong third place but moving up	**POV Curry**
Al wants to trade Isemonger, Curry discourages him	**POV Curry**
• add scene about Neal withholding story	**POV Linda**
Curry and Al watch game in which Isemonger sabotages Linda's attempt to steal home	**POV Curry**
• insert second half of split flashback, Al, Curry, Amanda	**POV Al**

8) SINKER
Al fires manager, makes Zack manager	**POV Linda**
Locker room, Zack tells team what baseball is about	**POV Linda**

Pennant race getting hotter, Eagles

1 game out of first	**POV Curry**
Neal and Linda	**POV Linda**
Newspaper article reveals Al's reasons for signing Linda	**POV Linda**

9) TURNAROUND

Eagles in first place, but Linda leaves	**POV Curry**
Neal confronts Linda, why she has to play	**POV Neal**
Article by Neal	**POV Neal**
Curry and Linda meet in Neal's apartment	**POV Curry**
	CLIMAX
Curry in taxi POV Curry	**DENOUEMENT**

This constituted two pages of outline for a 300-page story. As you can see, this particular outline lists plot points, with the point of view changing between the four main characters. This outline worked extremely well for me: it achieved its purpose of allowing me to write the novel, part by part.

My outline for *Sound Proof* was, as I've stated, quite different. It's more of a synopsis than an outline, telling me what would happen in each chapter. For this, my second mystery, I wrote the entire outline before writing the novel. Doing so was hard work, but it made writing the novel much easier. In fact, the writing of the novel sailed along quite smoothly after I wrote the outline. Below are the first three chapters of the 28-chapter outline. As you can surmise when you read them, at this point (outline stage) I'm telling the story to myself. (See chapter twenty-five to understand what this means.)

Sound Proof Outline

MONDAY

Chapter 1

At the Midwest Music Madness Festival in downstate Illinois, Shelby Stubbs insults those who signed up for his class by ridiculing their playing or their non-traditional instruments. Private eye Frank Dragovic, hired by festival organizer Mary Ployd, observes: he is there to spot who has been stealing instruments.

Chapter 2

Working undercover as a carpenter and attending the African drumming class, Frank watches the Old Time Ensemble class taught in the big barn by Stubbs. Two of the five suspects are taking Stubbs' class. Lafayette Wafer plays the bowed psaltry; Fonnie Sheffler plays guitar. After leaving the class Frank wanders through the vendors' area, helps newcomer Jeff Glover set up his booth and eyes a pair of Glover's "best bones west of the Mississippi" for Suzanne. Raven Hook, who teaches autoharp, asks Frank to fix the door to the corncrib where Mary has relegated the autoharp class.

Chapter 3

Frank meets Cody Thompson, a ten-year-old, and his mother Tansy, one of the MMM cooks. The temperature gauge on the farmhouse stoop reads 92°. Somebody has left a blue wedge-shaped guitar case (with guitar) on the stoop. Frank reports to Mary, who tells him she's sure Raven is the thief. Frank argues with Mary, saying he should be working on the theft case full time, rather than taking a drumming class each afternoon, but Mary insists that part of the MMM experience is the music. Frank gives Suzanne the bones he bought her, they walk to Glover's booth, where Stubbs and vendor Kim Oberfeld are arguing over the price of her fiddles. Stubbs then goes to Glover's booth, where Vance Jurasek is examining a fiddle. Stubbs tries to take it from Vance, but in doing so Stubbs falls over backward, gasping for air. Raven quickly helps him up and takes him and his expensive fiddle into her air conditioned room in the farmhouse.

My *Sound Proof* outline totaled more than 5,000 words. The novel is 77,000 words long, which means that my outline was approximately 6.5% of the novel itself. Normally I don't write such long, detailed outlines. My custom is to write a few short words for each chapter, as I did with *She's on First*. But when writing mystery fiction I have a fear of leaving something critical out. Also, I feel a need to control pacing and to plant clues throughout and, as I stated, it's easy enough to pace the story and plant clues in an outline.

Rewriting

In order to write as good a book as you can, it helps to keep in mind that your first pass through the story is simply that: a first draft. There will be other drafts, often three, four, or five of them. It also helps to keep in mind something professional writers know: rewriting is not a dismal chore, but a bright *opportunity* — an opportunity to make your story better. Much better.

Working with Others

But how do you know what's needed to make your story better? If you belong to a critique group (I highly recommend belonging to a critique group of like-minded writers), your fellow writers will offer suggestions on where your plot doesn't make sense, or where they fail to understand character motivation, or where they question something else. Listen to what they have to say and consider making their suggested changes. Some suggestions for change, you will agree with immediately. Others you will resist totally. And still others will fall into the middle range: you aren't sure whether you should make them or not. Follow your instincts. Definitely make the changes you agree with, resist the ones you suspect will not improve your story. As for the middle ones, maybe go partway: make some of them, don't make others.

If you don't belong to a critique group, then you might consider asking friends and acquaintances to read your manuscript. But beware: if your story is being read by people who are uncritical in their judgement (and usually non-writers are uncritical about story, structure, and language), you won't get much help from these people. Chances are they want to please and will say they love your story. They aren't able to help you improve it. So while you *can* ask friends and acquaintances to read your manuscript, that's the least successful route to go.

You could pay an editor to read your manuscript. There are freelance editors everywhere, and especially in this age of self-publishing it's easy to find them online. Before you agree to use one of these freelance editors, ask to see a sample of their critique work. You don't want to end up paying somebody $400-$1,000 for superficial comments about your work. Ask for the names of people for whom they've edited books and check with a few of those people to see if they were satisfied.

Although I've never worked with a freelance editor, I have worked with agents and with editors at publishing houses, and I've found that their comments and suggestions are usually quite astute. These people read — critically — hundreds of stories a year. They know what works and what doesn't. Most importantly, they know how to communicate to you, the writer, what needs to be done.

In addition to any one of these routes, you could buy and carefully read a book on self-editing for fiction writers. An online search will reveal that there are several such titles out there. You're better off reading two than you are reading one: you'll see two different approaches, and one will probably work better for you than the other. One of the self-editing books I highly recommend is *Self-Editing for Fiction Writers,* by Renni Browne and Dave King.

Read the self-editing book or books and take notes as you do so. By reading such books you'll be teaching yourself better writing skills. This means that with each successive novel you write, you will write a better story: one that will require fewer changes in the rewrite.

Rewriting in Stages

Once you recognize that you *must* rewrite and, hopefully, that you *want* to rewrite in order to improve your first draft, the question becomes: *how* do you rewrite? What's the best approach? The big danger in rewriting is to make what are called cosmetic changes: a word here, a phrase there, perhaps a deleted paragraph or two. Cosmetic changes do not constitute a rewrite: they constitute a touchup on something that remains essentially the same as it was before you applied the touchup.

An actual rewrite, on the other hand, tackles big problems in the manuscript if they need tackling. An important rewrite might include cutting the manuscript from 450 pages to 320 pages, for example. It might include building better characters and motivations. It might include adding a character, deleting one, merging two into one. Or perhaps changing the method of murder. Or the motive for it. Or the murderer. Perhaps the rewrite consists of a change in the point of view, which means that everything will be visualized and written in a new way.

The question is, how do you handle a rewrite if the needed changes overwhelm you? If they seem to be coming at you from all directions? Basically, there are two approaches. Each requires a *plan*.

The first plan is to tell yourself that you can't handle everything at once, so you will divide it into two or three stages, one rewriting per stage. Choose what you will handle in each of the rewrites. For example, you might decide that in the first rewrite you're going to deal with three very large issues: character, motivation, and plot. If so, sit down with a red (or blue, green, purple, whatever) pen and your manuscript and read your story as if somebody else wrote it and you are merely a reader trying to help that person improve the story. Write on the pages wherever you think you need to improve your presentation of characters, plot, or motivation. Then rewrite the story according to those notes. That finishes your second draft.

After you write your second draft you might then be looking to improve, say, narrative and scenes. That's a big job. Or you could work on setting and dialogue. Once again, go through the manuscript and write on the pages, indicating where you want to make changes. As you can infer, I do my rewriting on hard copy, not on screen. I do this because reading hard copy is slower than is reading text on screen, and because it's slower I notice more. Hard copy makes me a more critical reader. Also, if you're a person who reads books as opposed to ebooks, you'll find that reading a hard copy of your manuscript more closely approximates reading it in book form. I believe that sitting down with a pen and manuscript in hand makes you think more critically — more like a reader. Sitting in front of the computer screen makes you think more like a writer. And before you approach this draft as a writer, you want to have analyzed it as a reader and editor.

That third draft may be all you need. But if you're concerned with writing well, you might want to give the story one more rewrite. See the last chapter of this book.

Many Colors of Ink

When I first started writing fiction, I used the method explained above: I allotted myself two or three rewrites, each one tackling certain big problems in the manuscript, always moving from the largest problems down to smaller ones. However, after I wrote my first two novels (*She's on First* and *Dirty Proof*) I had gained enough experience to tackle rewriting in a different way, and that's the method I've been using ever since.

This method involves printing out a hard copy of the manuscript, sitting in a comfortable chair, and having at my side a pen in red, green, or purple ink. (I choose whichever color appeals to me that day.) What I do then is read the manuscript with, say, a red pen in hand, looking for places to improve on character, motivation, and plot. I make notes in red ink. As I read, I'm thinking only of character, motivation, and plot. I'm not thinking about other things that may need improving.

The next day, I sit down again with the same hard copy and take up another pen, perhaps purple. I then read critically, looking for places to improve narrative, scenes, and setting. Having finished that, I usually rewrite the manuscript in one go-through, incorporating the two different sets of changes, each set recorded in a different color of ink.

After the second draft is finished, I sit down yet again, this time with a freshly printed copy of the story and a new color of ink. This time I go through the manuscript looking for a way to make the writing better — that is, the sentences, and words themselves. More about this in the final chapter. And that comes next!

25 Writing Well

In writing circles it's said that each writer writes a story three times. First, she writes to tell the story to herself. Once she knows what the story is, then in the second effort she writes to tell that story to the reader. And in the third effort she writes the story in a literary manner. When I share this anecdote with students, I always tell them that the *three* is not to be taken literally. The three attempts may end up totaling five drafts. Or seven. Or just three. Generally, you can't move from one stage to the next until you've completed the stage you're in. That is, if you haven't written the story so that you know what it's all about, you can hardly proceed to tell the story to the reader in such a way that he knows what it's about. And you probably have no time or inclination to think about telling the story in a literary manner, because you don't know what the story is.

The reason for learning to write well is the same as the reason for learning to skate well if you intend to do so in public: so that you will move across the ice with power and grace . . . rather than draw stares and laughter because you keep tangling your feet and skates together and falling on your face.

What I advocate for those who want to tell a story in a literary manner is to concentrate on three aspects of language in that third phase of storytelling: (a) sentence structure; (b) word usage: (c) figurative language. In your first and probably second drafts you may be totally unaware of these things because you're concentrating on big problems such as character, motivation, and plot. But then comes the time for that third phase, when you look to improve the sentences and words you have written.

Sentence Types

In English there are four basic types of sentences: Simple, Compound, Complex, and Compound-Complex. In order to give your writing a pleasant movement and rhythm, learn to vary your sentence structure.

> **Simple Sentence** — Single subject and single predicate.
> **Hannah waited on the balcony.**
>
> **Compound Sentence** — Two or more independent clauses.
> **Hannah waited on the balcony, but the cat burglar failed to see her.**
>
> **Complex Sentence** — One independent clauses and one or more dependent clauses.
> **As the old tower clock struck two a.m., Hannah waited on the balcony.**
>
> **Compound-Complex Sentence** — A compound sentence with one or more dependent clauses.
> **As the old tower clock struck two a.m., Hannah waited on the balcony, but the cat burglar failed to see her until it was too late.**

Reprinted below are several consecutive paragraphs from *Sound Proof*. First read the paragraphs for pleasure, as if you're reading them in the novel.

> Up until last week I'd had no suspect list at all because the only thing I knew about Mary Ployd was that she was a folk singer from the Sixties. Old ballads came to mind, stories of lust, betrayal, murder. She had faded from sight until a couple of years ago, when she reemerged with a new song, "Jealous Man." Although Mary was a good singer with a deep, husky voice, it was the song more than the singer that grabbed public attention. At least one performer in every genre you can think of covered the song — country-western, bluegrass, rock, rhythm and blues, maybe even jazz and pop. Probably not hip-hop, but I couldn't swear to it.
> Until Suzanne brought it to my attention, I hadn't known Mary Ployd lived in Illinois, owned a farm in Auralee in Iroquois County, ran a music festival, or needed the help of a private eye.
> Back when Suzanne had been a frizzy-haired four-year-old growing up on Madeline Island, Wisconsin,

Mary Ployd had been her preschool teacher and later her babysitter. Mary left Wisconsin, but she and Suzanne met up again at the Old Town School of Folk Music in Chicago. Mary told Suzanne her problems, and Suzanne called me.

Anything I could do that would help Suzanne, I would. My good deed might even persuade her to move in with me, which I'd been urging for weeks. Or me with her. I wasn't particular about where. It was Suzanne I wanted.

Now look at the paragraphs again, as reproduced below. I've boldfaced the simple sentences and underlined the compound sentences. The complex sentences are in italics. There are no compound-complex sentences in this selection.

Up until last week I'd had no suspect list at all because the only thing I knew about Mary Ployd was that she was a folk singer from the Sixties. **Old ballads came to mind, stories of lust, betrayal, murder.** *She had faded from sight until a couple of years ago, when she reemerged with a new song, "Jealous Man." Although Mary was a good singer with a deep, husky voice, it was the song more than the singer that grabbed public attention.* **At least one performer in every genre you can think of covered the song — country-western, bluegrass, rock, rhythm and blues, maybe even jazz and pop.** <u>Probably not hip-hop, but I couldn't swear to it.</u>

Until Suzanne brought it to my attention, I hadn't known Mary Ployd lived in Illinois, owned a farm in Auralee in Iroquois County, ran a music festival, or needed the help of a private eye.

Back when Suzanne had been a frizzy-haired four-year-old growing up on Madeline Island, Wisconsin, Mary Ployd had been her preschool teacher and later her babysitter. <u>Mary left Wisconsin, but she and Suzanne met up again at the Old Town School of Folk Music in Chicago.</u> <u>Mary told Suzanne her problems, and Suzanne called me.</u>

Anything I could do that would help Suzanne, I would. *My good deed might even persuade her to move in with me, which I'd been urging for weeks.* **Or me with her.** **I wasn't particular about where.** **It was Suzanne I wanted.**

If you agree that the sentences and paragraphs as you first read them (before I marked them up) read well, then you can agree that *part* of what makes them flow is that the sentences aren't monotonous: they vary in structure. Varying your sentence structure is something you can learn to do. When going through your draft, simply decide to write at least one "varied" sentence per page. Figure out which sentence can best be changed for variety, then change it. Doing just this one thing — a sentence per page — will help your writing sound more interesting. And if you want, you can change the structure of two sentences a page. After a while, writing with different types of sentences will become so natural to you that you won't have to look for variety when rewriting: the variety will already be there.

Note, also, that certain sentence types seem appropriate to certain situations. In an action scene, you would naturally use short, simple sentences to help convey haste and intensity. Short simple sentences can convey emotion, as in the last sentence of my example, where Frank makes it clear, "It was Suzanne I wanted."

Compound sentences, complex sentences, and compound-complex sentences, on the other hand, are used to convey complex ideas or situations in which events, motives, and analyses are entangled. The second paragraph of the excerpt conveys the interconnectedness of events in Frank's mind.

Word Usage

When most people think of "word usage" they think of using a fancier, ten-dollar word in place of a common one. But that's not what writers mean by word usage. We mean that you should use the best word for what you're saying. Oftentimes that best word is a short word, often of Anglo-Saxon origin. For instance, the word *foe* conveys far more power and emotion than does the longer word *enemy*. And both words convey more emotion than *competitor* or *adversary*. That's because words of Anglo-Saxon origin (*foe*) are more visceral and less "removed" than are words of French or Latin origin. For a profound reading experience that conveys the power of Anglo-Saxon words, read the for-all-ages book, *Beowulf: A Hero's Tale Retold,* by James Rumford. When I read the first few pages to students, they are awe-struck — and they realize how very important word choices are.

The most important word in any sentence is the verb: verbs are action words, telling what is being done or happening. English contains a long list of overused verbs that we rely on. But we shouldn't, for these words are so *broad* in meaning that they pack no punch at all. All the "verbs of being" fall into this category: *is, has, was, were*, etc. So do words such as *get* or *put*. Look these up in a dictionary and you'll see they have more meanings than you would have thought possible. And none of the meanings are sharp.

So when you're sitting in that comfortable chair, pen in hand, scan the verbs on every page. When you see a weak verb, circle it. In the rewrite, replace that weak verb with a stronger, more exact one.

And speaking of exactness, readers will enjoy your writing more if they can "see" things. So learn the exact words or phrases for anything you might be describing. And remember that your detective (amateur, private, police) is observant. Here's an excerpt from *Sound Proof*.

> The bowed psaltry was shaped like a long isosceles triangle. I didn't know if psaltries came in sizes or not. Lafayette's was about two feet high, maybe eight inches wide, two inches deep. A string ran from the apex of the triangle to the base, with other strings following to the left and right. Each string was attached to a silver peg at its top end and an identical silver peg at its bottom, resulting in rows of silver pegs down the two long sides of the triangle. Shelby Stubbs had called the instrument a Christmas tree gone bad.

Notice that Frank describes the bowed psaltry in such a way that, if you ever saw one, you would recognize it. He doesn't say that it's shaped like a triangle: there are several different kinds of triangles. He observes that it's shaped like a *long isosceles triangle*. Its two identical sides are tall, or long. He then gives approximate dimensions. When he describes how the bowed psaltry is strung, he doesn't say "from top to bottom." Instead, he says that the strings run from *the apex of the triangle* to its base. *Isosceles, apex, base, silver pegs* — these are all exact words of description that help paint a vivid picture.

The quoted passage, by the way, is an example of exposition — information the reader needs in order to understand the story (in this case, in order to understand what a bowed psaltry is). I tried to add interest to the exposition by having Frank connect his description to Shelby Stubbs' humorous but nasty remark.

Figurative Language

As you go through each page of your manuscript varying sentence structure and replacing weak or inexact words with strong ones, also think about figurative language and try to employ it. Maybe not as often as once a page, but maybe at least one figurative expression every third or fourth page. Figurative expressions (those in which words are used beyond their literal meaning) bring writing to life.

Don't strive too hard to be clever about using metaphors or similes or idioms. It's often painful to read language that is too clever, too often, and calls attention to itself. Some hard-boiled novels are like this: it's as if the detective hero would die if he couldn't speak in witty figurative language with every utterance.

But employing figurative language here and there, several times a chapter, makes readers appreciate the writing. And when you do employ figurative language, make it fit the person who's using it.

Here are a few similes (comparison using *like* or *as*) from *Sound Proof*. They are of course all from the point of view of Frank Dragovic and thus not only help give the story some life, but help characterize Frank.

> The clicking and clinking of bones in the barn sounded like a ghostly echo of the hammers that had built the structure long ago.

> The first four steps weren't that bad. Like stepping into a pugnacious, overweight waterfall.

> He jumped a mile, stood facing me with his fiddle behind him, his bow thrust forward like a sword.

> What it looked like was a rummage sale on straw:

entire bales, sections of bales, and forked loose straw were all mixed up below.

Looking for evidence of a scuffle here was like listening for one drum beat in a thousand.

She planted the handle of the pitchfork on the ground and stood there like half of *American Gothic*.

Before I could do anything about it, Richard stormed straight into the tent area and through Vance's tent like a freight through match sticks.

Whatever your inclinations or attitudes towards writing well, I hope this chapter makes you want to try at least one of my suggestions: varying sentence structure, replacing weak words with strong ones, and using figurative language.

And I hope that the advice in this book helps you with your writing: with conceptualizing a mystery you may have in mind, with improving the complications of that mystery, and with telling the story in an satisfying way.

May you write mysteries that readers enjoy!

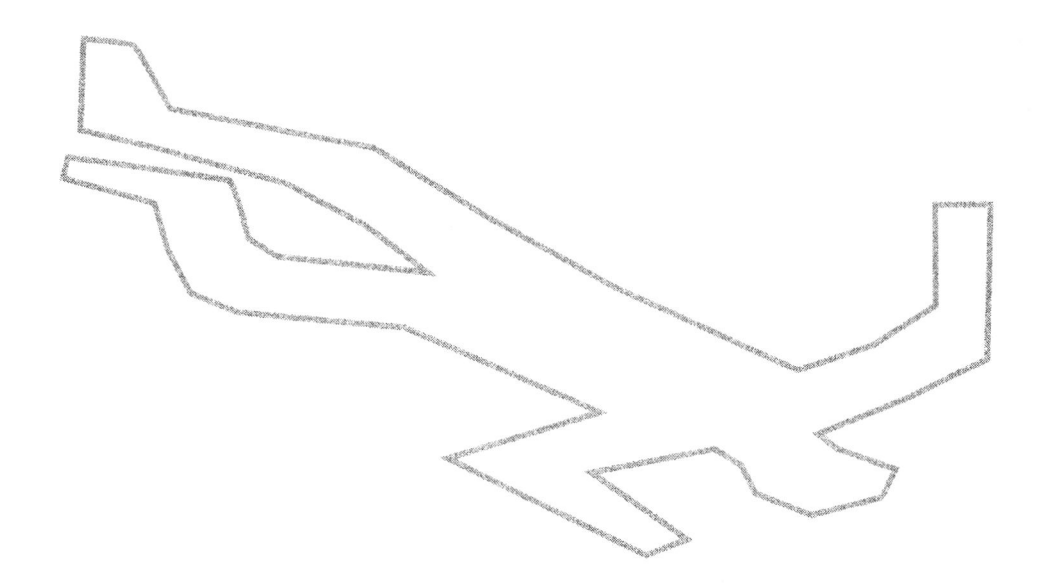

Index

A
Amateur detectives, 2-3, 9, 13, 45, 71
Antagonist, 6, 153. *See also* Villain

B
Beginnings, 151-152
Beginnings, Middles, and Ends (Kress), 151
Beowulf: A Hero's Tale Retold (Rumford), 204
Biggers, Earl Derr, 5, 22
Blackmail, as motive, 124
Blake, William, 17
The Blithedale Romance (Hawthorne), 78
Brother Cadfael novels (Peters), 126
Browne, Renni, 198
Building Better Plots (Kernen), 11-12, 94

C
Casting suspicion, 106-114
  back-and-forth vs. linear, 112-113
  means, 110-111, 125-127
  motive, 107-110, 122-124
  opportunity, 111-112, 125
  in *Sound Proof*, 113-114
Cause and effect, 10-11
Character development, 1, 30-43
  borrowing real-life characters, 30-32
  character traits, 35-37
  dialogue and, 163-168
  external characteristics, 32-34
  legal considerations, 30-32
  motivation, 37-39
  personality, 34-35
  from the subconscious, 39-43
Characters. See Character development; Character tags; Minor characters; Naming characters
Character tags, 50-56

for character traits, 53-55
as identification, 50-53
tension and, 55
Charlie Chan mysteries (Biggers), 5, 22
Christie, Agatha, 79, 116
Clues, 115-121
burying and deflecting, 120-121
number of, 115-117
in *Sound Proof*, 116, 117-120, 121
Complex sentence, 202
Compound-complex sentence, 202
Compound sentence, 202
Conflict, 5-7, 85-86
rising action and, 131
stating, with strong verbs, 7, 8
without dialogue, 90-92
Connelly, Michael, 79, 95
Cooper, Ablene, 31
Cozies. *See* Amateur detectives
Critique groups, 197
Cultural setting, 57, 58

D
Dactyls, 18
Denouement, 189-190
Description, 173-181
bad *vs.* good, 173-174
character tags, 50-53
figurative language, 178-181
observation with a purpose, 176-178
in *Sound Proof*, 174-178
Detectives
amateur, 2-3, 45
hard-boiled, 185, 206
police, 2, 9, 13, 65, 71
private eyes, 2-3, 9, 18, 37, 71
Dialogue
avoiding exposition in, 150-151
character development and, 163-168

oblique revelations through, 168-171
plot advancement through, 171-172
without conflict, 90-92
DiCamillo, Kate, 75
Dickens, Charles, 75
Dirty Proof (Gregorich)
character names in, 19-20
clues in, 121
conception of, 1-3
means in, 110
motive in, 108
multiple roles of characters, 6
murder plot point, 12
opportunity in, 111-112
scene of the crime, 65
setting, 58
suspects in, 107
villain of, 154, 183
Doyle, Arthur Conan, 78

E
Economic gain, as motive, 108, 123, 124
Edelstein, Linda N., 38
Ethnic names, 22-23
"Evangeline" (Longfellow), 18
Evidence, planting, 115-117
Exposition, 143-151
avoiding, in dialogue, 150-151
in *Sound Proof*, 143-150
weaving into story, 144-150

F
Family Names: The Origins, Meanings, Mutations, and History of More than 2,800 American Names (Hook), 23
Fer-de-Lance (Wolfe), 125
Figurative language, 178-181, 206-207
The Firm (Grisham), 79
First names. See under Naming characters
First person POV, 70-71

advantages and disadvantages of, 77-78
  first person multiple POV, 70
  first person plural POV, 71
  first person secondary-character POV, 78
  singular POV, 70, 96
  subplots and, 96-97
Fish, Stanley, 138
Fitzgerald, F. Scott, 78
Five Red Herrings (Sayers), 125
Foreshadowing, 157-162
  big events, 157-159
  minor characters, 161-162
  in *Soundproof*, 158-162
45 Master Characters: Mythic Models for Creating Original Characters (Schmidt), 38-39
Franklin, Jon, 7

G
Golden Age of mystery, 2, 110, 185
The Great Gatsby (Fitzgerald), 78
Grisham, John, 79

H
Hammett, Dashiell, 6
Hard-boiled detectives, 185, 206
Harry Bosch novels (Connelly), 79
Hawthorne, Nathaniel, 78
The Help (Stockett), 31
Hill, Antonio, 109
Hillerman, Tony, 23
Hines, Chester, 22
Hook, J. N., 23
How to Write a Sentence: and How to Read One (Fish), 138

I
Iambic pentameter, 16-17

J
James, P. D., 12, 137

Justice Hall (King), 123

K
Keating, H. R. F., 9
Kernen, Robert, 11-12, 94
King, Dave, 198
King, Laurie, 123
Kress, Nancy, 151

L
Lawsuits, avoiding, 30-32
Levithan, David, 71
Lickerman, Alex, 34, 35, 37
Longfellow, Henry Wadsworth, 18
"Lucy in the Sky with Diamonds," 18

M
The Maltese Falcon (Hammett), 6
The Man Who Loved Dogs (Padura), 137
McClanahan, Rebecca, 173
McDermid, Val, 125
Means of murder, 110-111
  disguising, 125-127
Metonymic names, 24
Minor characters, 44-49
  combining, 47-49
  foreshadowing and, 161-162
  function of, 45-47
  naming (or not), 44-45
Mirror, 6
Moby Dick (Melville), 6-7
Money (economic gain), as motive, 108, 123, 124
Motive, 107-110
  disguising, 122-124
  economic gain, 108, 123, 124
  protecting a secret, 108, 123
  revenge, 108, 109
  rivalry, 123, 124
  in *Sound Proof*, 124-125

Murder
  means, 110-111
  motive, 107-110, 122-125
  opportunity, 111-112
The Murder of Roger Ackroyd (Christie), 79

N
Naming characters, 16-29
changing names, 18-19
  connotations, 16
  ethnic names, 22-23
  examples, 16-20
  first names, 25-29
  minor characters, 44-45
  name origins (resources), 23-25
  rhythm of names, 16-18
  starting letters, 19-22
Narrative summary, 85, 89-90, 139-140
New Dictionary of American Family Names (Smith), 24
Notecard method (of plot development), 11-12

O
Opportunity for murder, 109, 111-112, 125
Outliers, 106
Outlining, 191-196
  She's on First sample, 192-194
  Soundproof sample, 194-196

P
Pace/pacing, 137-138
Padura, Leonardo, 137
Paretsky, Sara, 23
Passen, Phil, 3
Personalities, developing, 34-35. *See also* Character development
Peters, Ellis, 126
A Place of Execution (McDermid), 125
Plot, 1, 5-15. *See also* Subplots
  advancing through dialogue, 171-172
  basic questions of, 5

cause and effect, 10-11
complications, 101-105
number of suspects in, 9-10
plot points, 11-15
protagonists in, 7-8
purpose of scene, 86-89
spine of novel in, 7, 8-10
25-word summaries, 5-7
Point of view, 69-84
author's perspective of story, 81-82
avoiding violation of, 82-84
first person, 70-71, 77-78
preparing the reader, 80-81
second person, 76-77
subplots and (See under Subplots)
third person, 71-75
Police detectives/police procedurals, 2, 9, 13, 65, 71
Private detectives (private eyes), 2-3, 9, 18, 37, 71
Protagonist
conflict and, 6
driving force and plot, 7-8, 9
solution and, 182-183

R
Resolution, 6-8, 94-95
Revenge, as motive, 108, 109, 123
Rewriting, 197-200
different inks with various drafts, 200
plan, 199
in stages, 198-200
working with others, 197-198
Rising action, 131-138
Rivalry, as motive, 123, 124
Romance, 6
Rumford, James, 204

S
Sayers, Dorothy, 125, 126
Scene, 90-92, 140-141

Scene and plot
  improving, with summary, 89-90
  purpose of scene, 86-89
Scene of the crime, 65-68
Schmidt, Victoria Lynn, 38-39
Second person POV, 76-77
Secrets, as motive, 123
Self-Editing for Fiction Writers (Browne and King), 198
Sentence types, 201-204
Setting, 1, 57-68
  connections with, 63-65
  place, time, and culture, 57-58
  researching, 58-60
scene of the crime, 65-68
sketching, 60-63
Shakespeare, 17
Sherlock Holmes (Doyle), 79
She's on First (Gregorich)
  naming of character, 17-18
  point of view, 73-75, 80-81
  rising action in, 131
  working outline, 191-194
Simple sentence, 202
Smith, Elsdon C., 24
Solution
  protagonist and, 182-183
  revealing, 184-188
  tone of book and, 184
  villain and, 183-184
Sound Proof (Gregorich)
  character development, 32-39, 163-168
  character names, 20-22, 24, 25-28
  character tags, 51-55
  climax of, 185-189
  clues in, 116, 117-120, 121
  conception of, 3-4
  conflict in, 87-88
  early description in, 174-176
  exposition, 143-151

first person singular POV, 71
foreshadowing in, 158-162
introduction of villain, 154-156
means in, 111, 126
minor characters, 46-47, 155-156, 161-162
motives in, 108, 124-125
multiple roles of characters, 6
opportunity in, 112
plot complications, 102, 103-105
plot notes for, 10-11
plot points in, 12, 13-14
scene, 140-141
scene of the crime, 65-68
sentence types in, 202-203
setting, 58, 60-62, 64-65
spine of, 9
subplots in, 96-100
summary, 139-140
suspects in (casting suspicion), 106-107, 113-114
timelines, 128-130, 133-136
working outline, 14
Speech tags, 55-56
Spine of novel, 7, 8-10
Stockett, Kathryn, 31
Stout, Rex, 22, 137
Strong Poison (Sayers), 126
Strong verbs, 7-8, 180
Subconscious character development, 39-43
Subplots, 93-100
   first person POV and, 96-97
   number of, 93-95
   third person POV and, 95-96
Summary, 89-90, 139-140
   25-word plot summaries, 5-7
The Summer of Dead Toys (Hill), 109
Suspects. *See also* Clues
   casting suspicion, 106-114
   number of, 9-10

T

The Tale of Despereaux (DiCamillo), 75
Talking About Detective Fiction (James), 12
Tension
  character tags and, 55
  in climax of novel, 189
  foreshadowing and, 157
  number of suspects and, 9
  plot points and, 11
  rising action and, 131-132
Third person POV, 71-75, 79-80
  advantages and disadvantages, 79-80
  multiple POV, 95-96
  omniscient POV, 75
  subplots and, 95-96
  third person limited POV, 72
  third person multiple POV, 73
Through-line of novel, 9
Time, as setting, 57
A Time to Kill (Grisham), 79-80
Timelines, 128-130, 133-136
Tone, 184
Trochee, 16-17
Twain, Mark, 189-190
25-word plot summaries, 5-7
Two Boys Kissing (Levithan), 71

V

Verbs (strong verbs), 7-8, 180
Villain
  introducing, 153-156
  solution and, 183-184

W

Wolfe, Nero, 126
Word Painting: A Guide to Writing More Descriptively (McClanahan), 173
Word usage, 204-206
Writer's Guide to Character Traits (Edelstein), 38

Writing Crime Fiction (Keating), 9
Writing for Story (Franklin), 7
Writing the Blockbuster Novel (Zuckerman), 79
Writing well, 201-207
   figurative language, 206-207
   sentence types, 201-204
   word usage, 204-206

Z
Zuckerman, Albert, 79

About the Author

Barbara Gregorich was first published at the age of eleven. In her short poem titled "I Want a Horse," she carefully considered word choice and came up with *stamina*. She was next published at the age of sixteen, with a humorous memoir titled "Why I Hate Onions." Emboldened by those auspicious early publications, she has been writing ever since.

Her first adult fiction was the well-received novel, *She's on First*. This story of the first female major leaguer was praised by *Publishers Weekly*, which wrote that "all baseball fans will appreciate Gregorich's sure feel for the game . . . ." After writing the fictional version of women in baseball, Gregorich began the long job of researching the true story of women who played hardball. The result of that research was *Women at Play: The Story of Women in Baseball*, published by Harcourt, 1993. *Women at Play* won the SABR-Macmillan Award for Best Baseball Research of the Year. In 2013 *Women at Play* was included in Ron Kaplan's *501 Baseball Books Fans Must Read before They Die*.

Soon after the publication of her first novel, Gregorich published her second: a mystery titled *Dirty Proof*. After an interlude spent writing close to 200 educational works, she returned to mystery with the publication of *Sound Proof*.

When she isn't writing, Gregorich teaches seminars in writing fiction and nonfiction. She also goes to baseball games, hikes, and weaves baskets . . . steadfastly shunning onions but embracing mystery plots.

www.barbaragregorich.com

Printed in Great Britain
by Amazon